'Pooky Knightsmith is the measured, pragmatic voice of r(schools. If you're confused by the myriad options and opini.__ and you can't go far wrong. She is always coming from a place of pure kindness, ro~~ in a solid evidence base.'

– Natasha Devon MBE, Mental Health Campaigner

'Pooky champions everyone invested in the school environment! In this book she offers a clear and consistent way to develop a mentally healthy school; worksheets, action plans, tips and ideas, real-life experiences, inspiring quotes and suggestions for further reading are all offered in a genuine, supportive way. Pooky inspires you to make meaningful changes – as an individual as well as a team – that promote positive mental health in an educational setting and genuinely make a difference.'

– Helen Cossar, School Counsellor, Durham Schools Counselling Service

'Pooky never fails in giving sound, practical, useful advice based on the most current thinking on mental health. As a school counsellor, her books are my go-to whenever I doubt my interventions or need support with how to work with parents or staff in the school. I particularly like her "8 practical steps" in each chapter of how to make your school "mentally healthier" and her vision of long-term impact rather than quick fixes. A must-have on your shelf in the school counselling room. I look forward to changing mental health in schools with this tool.'

– Amy Hill, School Counsellor, Copthall School

'Pooky has been able to explain things in a clear, easy-to-understand format. The book has a whole-school approach and each chapter has ideas and action plans to challenge us. Many of these can be achieved almost immediately, and there are examples of excellent practice that can be cherry picked from and signposting for further reading. The litmus test includes everything you need to ensure a mentally healthy school and the self-care toolbox is essential.'

– Helen Lilley, Emotional Health Resilience Nurse

'Starting this book, I knew which chapters I most needed; on working my way through I was gently but firmly challenged in each of the six areas. This is a sensitive guide that enables honest reflection and has some great ideas. Our school already employs many of the schemes and strategies, but this framework has been brilliant for providing a "fresh eyes" review of where we are, where we want to be and most importantly a huge range of ways to get there. Clear and practical, well done Pooky! Top tip...never underestimate the power of a toilet door.'

– Jo Weaver, Senco, Devonport High School for Boys

'Pooky's book is an invaluable compendium of proactive ideas to make any school more mentally healthy. Say goodbye to hours wasted trying to collate resources because Pooky's book offers a concise, multifaceted approach in just 200 pages. I can really envision these ideas making school a better place for students like me.'

– Angelette Mendonca, Student, Henrietta Barnet School

'Key to this new workbook is the strive for small successful changes rather than aiming for big changes and not achieving them. Although aimed at senior leadership, this book is equally useful for practitioners and encourages small wins with little or no budget impact, as well as whole-school strategies. It was good to be reminded right at the start that staff wellbeing is at the heart of a mentally healthy school. This book has been written with this sentiment very much in mind. It is quick to read and easy to use. Each chapter follows the same simple format, so it is easy to go straight to the section that is going to be most helpful. Highly recommended for all levels of staff that are committed to becoming a mentally healthy school.'

– The Wellbeing Team, Uffculme School

THE MENTALLY HEALTHY SCHOOLS WORKBOOK

PRACTICAL TIPS, IDEAS, ACTION PLANS AND WORKSHEETS FOR MAKING MEANINGFUL CHANGE

POOKY KNIGHTSMITH

Foreword by Norman Lamb

Jessica Kingsley *Publishers*
London and Philadelphia

The text has been proofed in British English and internationalised terminology has been used throughout to ensure applicability to UK, US, Canadian and Australian readers.

First published in 2020
by Jessica Kingsley Publishers
73 Collier Street
London N1 9BE, UK
and
400 Market Street, Suite 400
Philadelphia, PA 19106, USA

www.jkp.com

Library of Congress Cataloging in Publication Data
Names: Knightsmith, Pooky, author.
Title: The mentally healthy schools workbook : practical tips, ideas and
    whole-school strategies for making meaningful change / Pooky Knightsmith.
Description: London ; Philadelphia : Jessica Kingsley Publishers, 2020.
Identifiers: LCCN 2019008642 | ISBN 9781787751484
Subjects: LCSH: Teachers--Mental health. | Students--Mental health. |
    Well-being.
Classification: LCC LB2840 .K555 2020 | DDC 371.7/13--dc23 LC
record available at https://lccn.loc.gov/2019008642

British Library Cataloguing in Publication Data
A CIP catalogue record for this book is available from the British Library

ISBN 978 1 78775 148 4
eISBN 978 1 78775 149 1

Printed and bound in Great Britain

For Colin – my childhood teacher and adult friend who caught me when I fell and continues to help me climb high. And for Simon, my daughters' Year 4 teacher who makes them, and me, feel heard.

All of the worksheets marked with ⭐ can be photocopied or downloaded from www.jkp.com/voucher using the code NEALEME.

Contents

Foreword

If you work in a school, the mental health of your students can seem like a really daunting issue.

For one thing, the prevalence of mental ill health and mental distress among children and young people is rising. When I was Minister, I secured funding for the Mental Health of Children and Young People Survey, which was released in November 2018. The statistics were shocking: one in eight students suffer from a mental health disorder, and this compares to one in ten from the previous survey which was conducted in 2004.

Young people face pressures which older generations haven't had to experience. The world of social media can be a force for good. But in many ways, it has led to people feeling more isolated than ever before. And while in the past, going home was sometimes a refuge for children after unpleasant days or experiences at school, today bullying doesn't stop at the school gates. It can continue right into the home and through the night thanks to social media.

There's never been a more pressing need for schools to develop their practice to promote positive mental health. But they face limited funding, over-stretched CAMHS services, and a lack of expertise. It can be difficult to know where to start. What can you do to help when the issues at hand are so huge?

I think there's reason to be optimistic. There is so much that you can do. Schools have a fantastic opportunity to bring about a positive change.

Prevention is a great example of this. It is so much better if we can stop people's mental health from deteriorating in the first place. It's particularly important when it comes to children, because an estimated 75 per cent of mental health problems experienced by adults start to develop before the age of 18.

But helping to prevent deterioration of mental ill health can require small scale actions which can lead to big results. Encouraging open conversations about mental health, or simply letting students know that there is a network of support should they need it. These things can make a real difference.

Overcoming stigma is hugely important. Stigma can prevent children and young people from speaking out about their mental ill health. It's estimated that over a third of young people who suffer from mental ill health have experienced stigma. Worryingly, it's most commonly experienced in schools.

But the evidence is clear that creating an atmosphere in which students feel comfortable talking about their mental health can be extremely effective. It can make a huge difference. Crucially, this requires a change in culture. You don't need a great deal of money, or expertise. That is important to recognise – it means that everyone who works in a school has an opportunity to create positive change.

We should be aiming for a point where children will talk about their mental health as freely as they would do their physical health.

That's where what's inside the following chapters will be helpful. Pooky Knightsmith has brought together a whole host of ideas to improve the mental health of your school. The ideas will be useful both for staff and pupils. They're laid out in an accessible, ready-to-use way, with case studies which you can learn from.

I won't pretend that implementing these ideas will always go to plan, but Pooky's advice will help you deal with the various hurdles you encounter as you put these steps into action. She has a wealth of experience, which this book is testament to.

I hope that you will find these ideas incredibly useful, and that they might inspire you and your teaching colleagues to seize the very real opportunity to significantly improve your school's mental health.

Norman Lamb MP

Acknowledgements

My biggest thanks goes to you for reading this book and taking action. I work with incredible people like you every day and many of you have no idea of the impact of the work you do and the ripples that work has throughout the lifetimes of the children you support. If you're someone who cares about children and enables them to feel heard and supported then my hat goes off to you. It's people like you who make the biggest difference to people like me. I was once that lost, scared child and you made life more manageable.

A huge thanks to my network around the world who've contributed to this book, in particular thanks to the tweeters whose ideas make up the 'Ideas to cherry pick from' sections in each chapter:

@00sixpointfive, @1tometoday, @2106head, @2yorkshiregirls, @4heartsandminds, @adrienneKatz1, @ajjolley, @alisonbaker01, @alisonclarke14, @annatwis, @az2bw, @BAPsmom612, @bizzybeejo, @boospurgeon, @bowiejcecc, @bye_amanda, @calmlifetherapy, @cathlowther, @cathmoor, @challendr, @ChildSocInclude, @cjtyack, @curliclare, @dcpsdeputyhead, @deeburf, @drhcgriffiths, @ebookwoman, @fionammiles, @fruitsforest16, @geoffjames42, @glenn_mutual, @hannahmeidd8p, @harvey_cate, @hopeproject2016, @iphonesrippin, @jane_flynn, @jennyhillparker, @jobartkirklees, @k_athertonpsy, @kathie_rees, @kaymagpie, @kazzannesturmey, @kcs_moraleja, @kerilizhaw, @keziah70, @ktclifford10, @lolly1980s, @lucindapowell, @Lucym808, @lwhmusictherapy, @miss_m_lally, @mm684, @mobooboo2011, @moominmamac, @motherexia, @mrsptaylor, @munroaurora, @nickymfinney, @outdoorprescrip, @owenstaton, @phoenixeducati3, @pivotalpaul, @pixtink, @qmgs_pshe, @rhiannonjoslin, @rodey_82, @safernetwork, @sarahcombe, @sarahjanecritch, @smartkidzpl, @somparshare, @striposteacher, @sue_cowley, @suemoreton1, @susanwilson271, @tasfund, @teachpmld, @TheHeadsOffice, @thosethatcan, @ukpastoraleast, @vshotbolt, @wellbeingeduca1.

Thank you too to everyone who provided case studies and the many people who've shared the ideas they've tried as a result of the many talks and workshops I've given on this topic.

Of course, thanks also go to my daughters who are my reason to be; my husband whose kindness, patience and sense of fun keeps me going; and to my amazing network of online and offline friends, colleagues and supporters. Finally, thank you to my publishing family at Jessica Kingsley Publishers, and especially to Amy Lankester-Owen from whose suggestion this book was born.

Introduction

Before I say anything else, I just want to say thank you for taking an interest in making your school more mentally healthy. Regardless of where you sit in the school pecking order, there will be things you can do to improve the lives of your students. I've tried to include a wide range of practical ideas throughout this book – some are tiny things that anyone can do, some are bigger things that could be applied across groups of schools working together, and the rest sit somewhere in the middle. More than anything, this book is designed to empower you to do *something* – to realise that there are simple things you can do that will make a big difference.

The book is born of an idea I first shared when looking for a practical and accessible way to summarise a whole-school approach to mental health when presenting at a conference with a couple of hundred school leaders in the room. Having worked with thousands of schools during my career, I've got to a point where upon walking into a school I can quickly get a feel for how mentally healthy it is. I felt that if I could summarise and share how I come to that feeling it would be valuable for school staff who could try it for themselves; and so my six-statement litmus test was developed and was shared with those school leaders who, I'm pleased to say, loved it. The litmus test consists of six simple statements that anyone can apply to their school that will help give them a steer as to where their strengths and challenges lie when it comes to mental health and wellbeing.

The statements are:

* Staff at my school are happy and healthy

* My school feels safe and welcoming

* The voice of every learner is heard and valued

* We recognise and support our most vulnerable learners

* Parents and carers positively engage with my school

* Students, staff and parents seek help when needed

In Chapter 2 you'll do a health check of your school, looking at all of the litmus test statements to help you come to an understanding of where your current strengths and challenges lie. Then you can look at each area in more depth in Chapters 3 to 8 where you can work through ideas and action plans to empower you to make a commitment to take practical steps towards change.

I've tried to include a wide range of ideas in this book and am enormously grateful to my huge network of colleagues worldwide who've been so generous in sharing their ideas and experiences for this book. Every idea I share has worked for someone – but they won't work for everyone – so read each chapter with an open mind and commit to exploring the ideas that feel like a good fit for your school and ignore those that don't. You'll find that the book is peppered with quotes and ideas. Some are attributed, some are not. Many of the unattributed quotes are the results of informal conversations I've had in the course of my work supporting students, parents and school staff across the UK and beyond when delivering workshops and training.

I hope you find this book helpful – please jump right in and get started. I look forward to seeing well-thumbed copies with filled-out action plans and plenty of your own notes added during my travels.[1] More than anything, this book is designed to get you asking the right questions, to spark some ideas and to give you a starting point for meaningful change so please dive in, write all over it, give things a go and make a difference.

Good luck!

Pooky
@PookyH – Twitter and Instagram
pooky@inourhands.com
www.pookyknightsmith.com
www.youtube.com/pookyh

---

1   All of the worksheets provided in this book, marked with ⬧, can be photocopied or downloaded from www.jkp.com/voucher using the code NEALEME so that as well as (or instead of) writing in the book, you can photocopy and download them as often as you wish.

Chapter 1

START WITH YOU

Before you get into the nitty gritty of this book and think about the practical steps you can take to meet the mental health needs of the learners in your school, I invite you first to think of your own needs. We're not always very good at that; the teaching and caring professions are renowned for attracting people who are kind, caring, altruistic and often teetering on the edge of physical or emotional burnout – often because we care too much. We're often very good at looking after others, but less good at looking after ourselves. But we matter too.

Isn't it selfish to put myself first?

Looking after yourself isn't selfish; far from it. When we practise good self-care, we're acting as role models to the children in our care. Furthermore, when we look after ourselves well, we better enable ourselves to look after others – which is about as selfless as you can get. Besides which, if we don't take time to look after ourselves, it always catches up with us in the end – especially those of us who give of ourselves so freely in supporting others. In the end, we physically or mentally burn out, at best leaving us unable to be our best selves at home and work, and at worst forcing us to completely withdraw.

You are a role model

Ask yourself what lesson you are teaching to your students through your actions. You can work as hard as you like to put together comprehensive schemes of work and lesson plans that teach students about self-care; but if you don't practise what you preach, these lessons will often ring hollow.

> 'She was teaching us about the importance of sleep but she yawned her way through the whole thing!'

If you truly believe in the recommendations you're making to students and your students can see you living by those beliefs and ideas, they're more likely to listen and copy. The learning we impart to students goes far beyond timetabled teaching in the classroom – prioritising your own self-care is one way to encourage students to do the same for themselves.

Physical wellbeing

The easiest way to make a difference to mental health, either your own or that of your students, is to first tackle your physical health. Getting good, regular sleep, a varied diet and at least a little exercise can make a huge difference to how well we feel and can make everything feel just that little bit more manageable. Above anything else, being well rested, fed and exercised can promote our resilience and leave us better able to manage the ups and downs of day-to-day life – but as soon as one of these is out of kilter, we can begin to struggle.

It's easily said, but often harder done, with good intentions often falling by the wayside once school is in full swing and we find ourselves doing whatever is necessary to simply get through. Sometimes little changes can make a big difference though. Take a little time to honestly appraise how well (or not) you are looking after your own physical wellbeing using the 'Physical wellbeing review' worksheet on the next page; then consider if there are any small changes you could make – you'll find lots of suggestions on the 'Physical wellbeing – small changes' worksheet. You could also do this exercise with students.

Healthy coping

We all have different ways of managing the ups and downs of day-to-day life; and there will always be ups and downs. It's important to recognise this and to prepare for the times of turbulence during times of calm. I like to think of myself as having a healthy coping toolbox, which I top up when things are going well and which I draw on when things are going less well. We are much better able to cope during times of crisis if we've prepared ahead. Working in education, that usually means using the holidays or the weekends to think forwards towards the end of the next week or the last few weeks of term and thinking proactively about the things we can do to help ourselves overcome, or live with, difficult thoughts and feelings. As term wears on it's common to find that our mood dips or we feel more stressed or anxious – but if we've planned ahead and thought about the things that might help us and made a commitment to trying them, then in moments of crisis, our current stressed, anxious, low self doesn't have to do any thinking, we can just get on with doing the things we've pre-planned, and, we hope, end up feeling a whole lot better.

Use the 'Wellbeing action plan' from the end of this chapter to put together a plan that you can use to help you identify a range of ideas that could make up your healthy coping toolbox as well as recognising the warning signs that you're doing less well and when and how to seek help if things get especially difficult.

PHYSICAL WELLBEING REVIEW

SLEEP

Sleep is the cornerstone of wellbeing. When we've not had enough sleep we are less resilient, we make less good decisions and everything feels harder. Many of us are chronically sleep deprived. Are you? Think back over the last few weeks and consider whether you've had enough sleep in general. Be honest!

Write a little about your current sleep habits. When do you go to bed? When do you get up? You might like to consider:

- How many hours of sleep do you generally get?

- Is this enough? (How much sleep we need varies from person to person.)

- Does this vary at weekends or in the holidays?

- Do you wake up feeling refreshed?

- Are you tired during the day?

. . . .

. . . .

. . . .

. . . .

. . . .

. . . .

. . . .

Does anything need to change? For example, do you think you'd benefit from more or better-quality sleep?

. . . .

. . . .

. . . .

. . . .

. . . .

. . . .

. . . .

DIET

Most of us are aware that a balanced healthy diet will help to boost our wellbeing, but it can be hard to achieve during the busy school term. Think honestly about what and how you eat and whether you think that you'd benefit from any changes.

Write a little about your dietary habits. What, when and where do you eat?
You might like to consider:

- What does a typical food day look like?

- Do you eat more or less healthily at one particular mealtime?

- Where do you eat and who with?

- Do you have time for food prep and eating or are you always on the go?

- Are your food choices driven by what your body needs or other factors, for example what you have time to prepare/eat?

- Do you ever feel tired because you're either hungry or overfull?

- Are mealtimes a pleasure or a chore – and does this change, for example, at weekends or holidays?

....

....

....

....

....

....

....

Does anything need to change? For example, do you think you'd benefit from being able to slow down to eat, varying your diet or changing up your snacks?

....

....

....

....

....

....

PHYSICAL ACTIVITY

When we're busy with school, getting enough exercise can be difficult even if it's something we enjoy.

Write a little about your physical activity. This can include anything that gets you active even if it's not formal 'exercise', for example walking to the bus stop.

You might like to consider:

- How much physical activity do you get in a typical day?

- Are there any physical activities that you enjoy when you have more time, for example in the holidays?

- Are there little moments in the day when you get little bits of exercise?

- Are there any activities that bring you particular pleasure or which help with your mood?

. . . .

. . . .

. . . .

. . . .

. . . .

. . . .

. . . .

. . . .

Does anything need to change? For example, do you think you'd benefit from doing more physical activity or getting outside more?

. . . .

. . . .

. . . .

. . . .

. . . .

. . . .

. . . .

. . . .

PHYSICAL WELLBEING – SMALL CHANGES

If you identified that you'd like to make some changes with regard to your sleep, diet or physical exercise, have a think about small, sustainable changes you might be able to make. This isn't about overhauling your life overnight, it's about making small, tangible changes to help you feel a little better every day.

Try to commit to at least one small change; then stick with it for a week or two and review the impact. Try not to change too much at once or to set yourself goals that are too big – the key here is to think small and build on success. Successfully achieving an extra 15 minutes of sleep a night will be a bigger boost to your wellbeing than failing to achieve an extra hour.

SLEEP

I commit to trying to:

. . . .

. . . .

. . . .

. . . .

. . . .

. . . .

Start date: . . . .

Review date: . . . .

Notes:

. . . .

. . . .

. . . .

. . . .

. . . .

. . . .

DIET

I commit to trying to:

. . . .

. . . .

. . . .

. . . .

. . . .

. . . .

. . . .

. . . .

Start date: . . . .

Review date: . . . .

Notes:

. . . .

. . . .

. . . .

. . . .

. . . .

. . . .

. . . .

. . . .

PHYSICAL ACTIVITY

I commit to trying to:

. . . .

. . . .

. . . .

. . . .

. . . .

. . . .

. . . .

. . . .

Start date: . . . .

Review date: . . . .

Notes:

. . . .

. . . .

. . . .

. . . .

. . . .

. . . .

. . . .

. . . .

Sleep: ten small changes you could consider trying

- Set yourself regular bed and wake times

- Take a little time to make your bedroom feel like a calm place for sleep

- Ensure your bedroom is dark enough and cool enough for a good night's sleep

- Don't consume caffeine or sugar in the hours before bed

- Give yourself a few minutes to do a calming activity before bed

- Go screen free in the bedroom

- Charge your phone away from your bed

- Do a little exercise so that you feel physically as well as mentally tired

- Consider what you eat for dinner and when so that you don't go to bed overfull or hungry

- Finish working at a set time and give yourself time to wind down before bed

Diet: ten small changes you could consider trying

- Try to eat breakfast every day

- Prepare meals for the busy week ahead when you have a little more time at the weekend

- Take a few minutes to stop and eat lunch

- Buy and carry healthy snacks you enjoy

- Plan in treat meals that you really enjoy and take time to enjoy them

- If you live with others, sit down once a week and eat as a family

- Find a friend to eat with at school; talk about anything other than work

- Carry water and try to drink enough

- If you think you're consuming too much sugar, caffeine or alcohol, consider substitutes you could make to help you step down your consumption

- Make a meal plan before you do your shopping

Physical activity: ten small changes you could consider trying

- Add a little walking into your daily commute – even small steps like parking at the far end of the carpark can help increase your activity

- Suggest 'walking meetings' to colleagues – this helps you get active, can help ideas to flow and often shortens the length of meetings too!

- Consider fun activities you could do with friends or family such as going for a weekend bike ride

- Join students in doing the 'daily mile' – or introduce it if your school doesn't already participate – more here: https://thedailymile.co.uk

- Measure your daily steps and try to add a thousand to your daily average – competing with friends can make this more fun

- Join a class or team – having a regular time and a group of people to exercise with will make you more likely to follow through

- If you don't like the idea of a class, consider finding videos so you can exercise at home – I can highly recommend Yoga with Adriene if you'd like free YouTube videos to get you started with yoga: www.youtube.com/yogawithadriene

- Start staff social teams – for example, netball, football or any other sport you fancy; play just for fun, perhaps against students or, if there's enough interest, in a staff league or cup

- Find a dog or a friend to walk with – commit to walking regularly

- Try out a completely new sport together with a friend – I can recommend indoor bouldering (climbing without ropes) as a brilliant sport that is widely available, great fun and a mental as well as a physical challenge.

WELLBEING ACTION PLAN

You'll get the most from your wellbeing action plan if you spend a little time on it when you're feeling relatively calm; think of it as planning ahead for stormy weather whilst the sun is shining. This doesn't need to be perfect; often the first ideas that come to mind are the best ones. Over time you might choose to add to and update it; it's not designed to be cast in stone, but rather a starting point for staying well and seeking help when needed.

HEALTHY COPING TOOLBOX

Use this space to record as wide a range of ideas as you can think of that help to keep you well. Add to it over time. It can be anything from going for a run, having a cup of tea, drawing, listening to music, chatting to a friend and so on and so on.

. . . .

. . . .

. . . .

. . . .

. . . .

. . . .

. . . .

THINGS TO DO EVERY DAY

What are the things you should commit to doing every day to keep well? You might think here about the basics of sleep, food and exercise as well as considering what you can do each day to spark a little joy.

. . . .

. . . .

. . . .

. . . .

. . . .

. . . .

. . . .

THINGS TO AVOID EVERY DAY

On the flip side, what are the things you want to commit to not doing, in order to maintain your wellbeing? Mine include not comparing myself to others on social media, not drinking to excess and not self-harming; yours may be very different.

. . . .

. . . .

. . . .

. . . .

. . . .

WARNING SIGNS

What are the tell-tale warning signs that you're doing less well? You can become more attuned to these over time. It can be incredibly helpful to keep an eye out for them and take proactive steps to look after yourself before your mental health dips too far. Lots of people find that their appetite or sleep patterns change when their mood is dipping; for me an overfull inbox and a phone full of unanswered text messages is a warning sign that I need to take action.

. . . .

. . . .

. . . .

. . . .

. . . .

NEXT STEPS

If you spot your warning signs, what are your next steps? Who can you talk to? What can you do to look after yourself? Think about your support network as well as the self-care steps you might need to take.

. . . .

. . . .

. . . .

. . . .

. . . .

Chapter 2

HOW MENTALLY HEALTHY IS YOUR SCHOOL?

Before you decide what steps you need to take to make your school mentally healthy, it's time to step back and honestly appraise how things are currently going. This gives you a baseline to work from and a clear idea of your current strengths and challenges. Be as honest as you can and remember that, with a little work, your current weaknesses may become your future strengths.

This doesn't need to take long – people's gut reactions are usually the best reactions. I've provided several copies of the litmus test audit so you can record scores from a range of people. It can be helpful to revisit this exercise once you feel you've made some progress to see if others agree too.

For each of the items in my litmus test, rank yourself from 1 to 10 – where 1 signifies 'not at all' and 10 signifies 'completely'. If possible, you should then go and ask the same questions of a range of people who will give you some honest answers and provide a different point of view. Ideally you would ask as many of the following as possible:

* A student from each year group

* Students from vulnerable or minority groups

* Parents and carers who are engaged with the school

* Parents and carers who are currently less engaged (not easy!)

* A governor

* A member of support staff

* A member of teaching staff

* A middle leader

* A senior leader

GOALies

This is even better if you can appoint 'GOALies' from each of these groups – 'GOALies' Go Out And Listen to others like them – so the score from the support staff GOALie would represent the feeling of support staff as a whole. Having a team of people you can regularly turn to for honest feedback during the process of trying to make your school more mentally healthy is a hugely valuable resource. That said, it's better to do something than nothing, so don't let the fact you're unable to instantly recruit a team of GOALies put you off moving forwards with the book. Even just spending five minutes recording your own scores will give you a decent starting point.

We've provided space for ten people to complete a baseline audit of your school on the following pages.

NOTES:

....

....

....

....

....

....

....

....

....

....

....

....

....

....

....

MENTALLY HEALTHY SCHOOL AUDIT

Date: . . . .   Name: . . . .   Role: . . . .

1. Staff at my school are happy and healthy

1	2	3	4	5	6	7	8	9	10

Notes:

. . . .

. . . .

. . . .

. . . .

2. My school feels safe and welcoming

1	2	3	4	5	6	7	8	9	10

Notes:

. . . .

. . . .

. . . .

. . . .

3. The voice of every learner is heard and valued

1	2	3	4	5	6	7	8	9	10

Notes:

. . . .

. . . .

. . . .

. . . .

4. We recognise and support our most vulnerable learners

1	2	3	4	5	6	7	8	9	10

Notes:

. . . .

. . . .

. . . .

. . . .

5. Parents and carers positively engage with my school

1	2	3	4	5	6	7	8	9	10

Notes:

. . . .

. . . .

. . . .

. . . .

6. Students, staff and parents seek help when needed

1	2	3	4	5	6	7	8	9	10

Notes:

. . . .

. . . .

. . . .

. . . .

MENTALLY HEALTHY SCHOOL AUDIT

Date: . . . .   Name: . . . .   Role: . . . .

1. Staff at my school are happy and healthy

1	2	3	4	5	6	7	8	9	10

Notes:

. . . .

. . . .

. . . .

. . . .

2. My school feels safe and welcoming

1	2	3	4	5	6	7	8	9	10

Notes:

. . . .

. . . .

. . . .

. . . .

3. The voice of every learner is heard and valued

1	2	3	4	5	6	7	8	9	10

Notes:

. . . .

. . . .

. . . .

. . . .

4. We recognise and support our most vulnerable learners

1	2	3	4	5	6	7	8	9	10

Notes:

. . . .

. . . .

. . . .

. . . .

5. Parents and carers positively engage with my school

1	2	3	4	5	6	7	8	9	10

Notes:

. . . .

. . . .

. . . .

. . . .

6. Students, staff and parents seek help when needed

1	2	3	4	5	6	7	8	9	10

Notes:

. . . .

. . . .

. . . .

. . . .

MENTALLY HEALTHY SCHOOL AUDIT

Date: . . . .   Name: . . . .   Role: . . . .

1. Staff at my school are happy and healthy

1	2	3	4	5	6	7	8	9	10

Notes:

. . . .

. . . .

. . . .

. . . .

2. My school feels safe and welcoming

1	2	3	4	5	6	7	8	9	10

Notes:

. . . .

. . . .

. . . .

. . . .

3. The voice of every learner is heard and valued

1	2	3	4	5	6	7	8	9	10

Notes:

. . . .

. . . .

. . . .

. . . .

4. We recognise and support our most vulnerable learners

1	2	3	4	5	6	7	8	9	10

Notes:

....

....

....

....

5. Parents and carers positively engage with my school

1	2	3	4	5	6	7	8	9	10

Notes:

....

....

....

....

6. Students, staff and parents seek help when needed

1	2	3	4	5	6	7	8	9	10

Notes:

....

....

....

....

MENTALLY HEALTHY SCHOOL AUDIT

Date: . . . . Name: . . . . Role: . . . .

1. Staff at my school are happy and healthy

1	2	3	4	5	6	7	8	9	10

Notes:

. . . .

. . . .

. . . .

. . . .

2. My school feels safe and welcoming

1	2	3	4	5	6	7	8	9	10

Notes:

. . . .

. . . .

. . . .

. . . .

3. The voice of every learner is heard and valued

1	2	3	4	5	6	7	8	9	10

Notes:

. . . .

. . . .

. . . .

. . . .

4. We recognise and support our most vulnerable learners

1	2	3	4	5	6	7	8	9	10

Notes:

....

....

....

....

5. Parents and carers positively engage with my school

1	2	3	4	5	6	7	8	9	10

Notes:

....

....

....

....

6. Students, staff and parents seek help when needed

1	2	3	4	5	6	7	8	9	10

Notes:

....

....

....

....

MENTALLY HEALTHY SCHOOL AUDIT

Date: . . . .   Name: . . . .   Role: . . . .

1. Staff at my school are happy and healthy

1	2	3	4	5	6	7	8	9	10

Notes:

. . . .

. . . .

. . . .

. . . .

2. My school feels safe and welcoming

1	2	3	4	5	6	7	8	9	10

Notes:

. . . .

. . . .

. . . .

. . . .

3. The voice of every learner is heard and valued

1	2	3	4	5	6	7	8	9	10

Notes:

. . . .

. . . .

. . . .

. . . .

4. We recognise and support our most vulnerable learners

1	2	3	4	5	6	7	8	9	10

Notes:

. . . .

. . . .

. . . .

. . . .

5. Parents and carers positively engage with my school

1	2	3	4	5	6	7	8	9	10

Notes:

. . . .

. . . .

. . . .

. . . .

6. Students, staff and parents seek help when needed

1	2	3	4	5	6	7	8	9	10

Notes:

. . . .

. . . .

. . . .

. . . .

MENTALLY HEALTHY SCHOOL AUDIT

Date: . . . .   Name: . . . .   Role: . . . .

1. Staff at my school are happy and healthy

1	2	3	4	5	6	7	8	9	10

Notes:

. . . .

. . . .

. . . .

. . . .

2. My school feels safe and welcoming

1	2	3	4	5	6	7	8	9	10

Notes:

. . . .

. . . .

. . . .

. . . .

3. The voice of every learner is heard and valued

1	2	3	4	5	6	7	8	9	10

Notes:

. . . .

. . . .

. . . .

. . . .

4. We recognise and support our most vulnerable learners

1	2	3	4	5	6	7	8	9	10

Notes:

....

....

....

....

5. Parents and carers positively engage with my school

1	2	3	4	5	6	7	8	9	10

Notes:

....

....

....

....

6. Students, staff and parents seek help when needed

1	2	3	4	5	6	7	8	9	10

Notes:

....

....

....

....

MENTALLY HEALTHY SCHOOL AUDIT

Date: . . . .   Name: . . . .   Role: . . . .

1. Staff at my school are happy and healthy

1	2	3	4	5	6	7	8	9	10

Notes:

. . . .

. . . .

. . . .

. . . .

2. My school feels safe and welcoming

1	2	3	4	5	6	7	8	9	10

Notes:

. . . .

. . . .

. . . .

. . . .

3. The voice of every learner is heard and valued

1	2	3	4	5	6	7	8	9	10

Notes:

. . . .

. . . .

. . . .

. . . .

4. We recognise and support our most vulnerable learners

1	2	3	4	5	6	7	8	9	10

Notes:

....

....

....

....

5. Parents and carers positively engage with my school

1	2	3	4	5	6	7	8	9	10

Notes:

....

....

....

....

6. Students, staff and parents seek help when needed

1	2	3	4	5	6	7	8	9	10

Notes:

....

....

....

....

MENTALLY HEALTHY SCHOOL AUDIT

Date: . . . .   Name: . . . .   Role: . . . .

1. Staff at my school are happy and healthy

1	2	3	4	5	6	7	8	9	10

Notes:

. . . .

. . . .

. . . .

. . . .

2. My school feels safe and welcoming

1	2	3	4	5	6	7	8	9	10

Notes:

. . . .

. . . .

. . . .

. . . .

3. The voice of every learner is heard and valued

1	2	3	4	5	6	7	8	9	10

Notes:

. . . .

. . . .

. . . .

. . . .

4. We recognise and support our most vulnerable learners

1	2	3	4	5	6	7	8	9	10

Notes:

. . . .

. . . .

. . . .

. . . .

5. Parents and carers positively engage with my school

1	2	3	4	5	6	7	8	9	10

Notes:

. . . .

. . . .

. . . .

. . . .

6. Students, staff and parents seek help when needed

1	2	3	4	5	6	7	8	9	10

Notes:

. . . .

. . . .

. . . .

. . . .

MENTALLY HEALTHY SCHOOL AUDIT

Date: . . . .   Name: . . . .   Role: . . . .

1. Staff at my school are happy and healthy

1	2	3	4	5	6	7	8	9	10

Notes:

. . . .

. . . .

. . . .

. . . .

2. My school feels safe and welcoming

1	2	3	4	5	6	7	8	9	10

Notes:

. . . .

. . . .

. . . .

. . . .

3. The voice of every learner is heard and valued

1	2	3	4	5	6	7	8	9	10

Notes:

. . . .

. . . .

. . . .

. . . .

4. We recognise and support our most vulnerable learners

1	2	3	4	5	6	7	8	9	10

Notes:

....

....

....

....

5. Parents and carers positively engage with my school

1	2	3	4	5	6	7	8	9	10

Notes:

....

....

....

....

6. Students, staff and parents seek help when needed

1	2	3	4	5	6	7	8	9	10

Notes:

....

....

....

....

MENTALLY HEALTHY SCHOOL AUDIT

Date: . . . .   Name: . . . .   Role: . . . .

1. Staff at my school are happy and healthy

1	2	3	4	5	6	7	8	9	10

Notes:

. . . .

. . . .

. . . .

. . . .

2. My school feels safe and welcoming

1	2	3	4	5	6	7	8	9	10

Notes:

. . . .

. . . .

. . . .

. . . .

3. The voice of every learner is heard and valued

1	2	3	4	5	6	7	8	9	10

Notes:

. . . .

. . . .

. . . .

. . . .

4. We recognise and support our most vulnerable learners

1	2	3	4	5	6	7	8	9	10

Notes:

. . . .

. . . .

. . . .

. . . .

5. Parents and carers positively engage with my school

1	2	3	4	5	6	7	8	9	10

Notes:

. . . .

. . . .

. . . .

. . . .

6. Students, staff and parents seek help when needed

1	2	3	4	5	6	7	8	9	10

Notes:

. . . .

. . . .

. . . .

. . . .

DRAWING ON OTHER DATA

If you've got other data you can draw on that feels relevant, make a note of the headlines here. This might include things like student, parent or staff surveys or feedback from inspection reports. Rough notes will do here – you're simply trying to build as complete a picture of your school as you can.

Notes:

. . . .

. . . .

. . . .

. . . .

. . . .

. . . .

. . . .

. . . .

. . . .

. . . .

. . . .

. . . .

. . . .

. . . .

. . . .

. . . .

. . . .

. . . .

. . . .

. . . .

Determine your priorities

Once you've had a chance to consider how your school scores against each of the litmus test areas, consider which areas are your priorities. You might choose to work on all six areas at once, but I'd recommend picking one or two areas to focus on at a time. Remember that your existing areas of weakness can become your future strengths with a little concerted effort. Equally, just because an area is one of existing strength doesn't mean that there isn't more to be done – and current successes to celebrate.

Before you move on, take a moment to consider the order in which you're going to tackle the six areas. Yes, I am giving you permission to read the book out of order! You can read it in any order you like and you can dip in and out as you please. This book should be your companion, your inspiration and your ideas depository as you work through the process rather than something you pick up, read cover to cover and file away.

So, pick the area you'd most like to work on and jump straight to that chapter and start collating ideas about your next steps.

Staff at my school are happy and healthy – Chapter 3

My school feels safe and welcoming – Chapter 4

The voice of every learner is heard and valued – Chapter 5

We recognise and support our most vulnerable learners – Chapter 6

Parents and carers positively engage with my school – Chapter 7

Students, staff and parents seek help when needed – Chapter 8

STAFF AT MY SCHOOL ARE HAPPY AND HEALTHY

Mentally healthy schools should not be places where children flourish at the expense of staff. Instead, they should be places where everybody's mental health matters and steps are taken to promote the physical and emotional wellbeing of staff as well as students.

You cannot pour from an empty cup

If we're going to be in a good position to support our students emotionally or academically, we need to be happy and healthy ourselves. If we continually give of ourselves but do not take the appropriate steps to guard our own wellbeing, we will eventually run out of steam. Conversely, if we practise self-care and take steps to promote our physical and mental health, we are more likely to be able to support our students, their parents and our colleagues. In a profession that attracts people who often tend towards altruism and determination, taking time to look after ourselves does not always come naturally. But it matters – and it matters for everyone from the most senior to the most junior staff.

TRY THIS?

'We have a wellbeing week every term where there are no after-school meetings and staff are actively encouraged to go home early and plan lessons that don't require marking, i.e. role play and art. It's lovely and really helps.' @moominmamac

Sustainable change must have staff at its heart

When I visit a school and I encounter staff who are happy, healthy and feel well supported in their work, I am more confident that any steps being taken to promote student wellbeing are not tokenistic. It is all very well putting policies in place, and posters on the walls – but real change happens when there is a belief in the process from the top down. It is very difficult to take the steps needed to change a school's culture and ethos if leaders aren't on board – everybody is a role model to somebody and it is incumbent on senior and middle leaders to inspire those they line manage to take appropriate steps to safeguard and promote their wellbeing. Bar none, the most powerful way of doing this is leading by example. A senior or middle leader who overtly practises self-care gives permission, through their actions, for more junior staff to do the same.

> 'The head said she wanted us all to try and have at least a few minutes' break at lunchtime. She suggested encouraging each other to stop to eat lunch – not to eat at our desks or on the go, but to give ourselves permission to have even the briefest of breaks and eat with colleagues in the staffroom. She always used to eat at her desk, if at all, but she started eating her lunch in the staffroom, encouraging others to join her, and she made a huge effort to drive the conversation onto anything other than work. It felt really weird at first, but we got the hang of it after a while.'

Conversely, we can lead by example when it comes to unhealthier habits too:

> 'My head of department sends emails every hour of the day and night. She says she doesn't expect us to read and respond at those times, but even though she says you don't have to read and reply, you kind of feel like you should – like if she's working at those times, I should be too...'

Our actions can really permeate and be a driver for change. It can take a little while, but a school where it is considered important that all staff take appropriate steps to promote their own health and happiness is often a key indicator of a school where students will, in turn, be happy and healthy too.

Staff are role models to students

A staff body that practises what it preaches is also often indicative of a school where staff genuinely believe in the importance of the lessons they are imparting to students with regard to mental health and wellbeing. When we walk the walk as well as talking the talk, it teaches a powerful lesson indeed; students learn from what we do as well as what we say, and we can quickly undermine messages about mental and physical health promotion if it is clear from our actions that we don't believe the lessons we're teaching. Instead, being able to explore these topics with students in an environment where we're all learning together, where everybody's wellbeing matters and where we, as well as them, consider and share the steps we need to take to better look after ourselves imparts a very valuable lesson.

> 'Our teacher joined in with the daily mile with us because he said that it's important for grown-ups to exercise too, not just children.'

One great thing about thinking of ourselves as wellbeing role models is that it can help us to overcome any feelings we might have that it is somehow selfish or inappropriate to put ourselves first. It's not, but it can be hard to undo a lifetime of putting other people's needs first. However, when we stop and realise the powerful lessons we teach our students by role modelling self-care, it can give us absolute permission to take the steps we need to promote our own wellbeing as we know that it is to the benefit of our students.

TRY THIS?

'We have secret buddies – they're someone to look out for you, drop you a word of encouragement, or even a small gift. No one has to join in, but most staff choose to.' @fionammiles

NOTES:

. . . .

. . . .

. . . .

. . . .

. . . .

. . . .

. . . .

. . . .

. . . .

. . . .

. . . .

. . . .

. . . .

COLLECTING IDEAS:
STAFF AT MY SCHOOL ARE HAPPY AND HEALTHY

This space is for you to jot down your thoughts and ideas as they arise. I've split it into start, stop, continue and change, which can be a neat way of thinking about the actions we need to take. You might make a few notes of things you learned during the Mentally Healthy School Audit/Go Out And Listen exercise (see the end of Chapter 2) or you could make notes of your ideas as you read this chapter. Revisit this space and keep track of additional ideas as they arise here. It's not meant to be perfect or beautiful, it's just a place to keep your ideas so you can refer to it when you do your action planning.

Things to START doing…

....

....

....

....

....

....

....

....

....

Things to STOP doing…

....

....

....

....

....

....

....

....

....

Things to CONTINUE doing...

. . . .

. . . .

. . . .

. . . .

. . . .

. . . .

. . . .

. . . .

Things to CHANGE our way of doing...

. . . .

. . . .

. . . .

. . . .

. . . .

. . . .

. . . .

. . . .

Other notes:

. . . .

. . . .

. . . .

. . . .

. . . .

. . . .

EIGHT PRACTICAL STEPS YOU COULD TAKE

The key is not to take all of these steps, but rather to identify a few that feel like a good fit and to focus on how you might go about achieving those. Use the action plan later in this chapter to help you.

1. Start with you and write a personal wellbeing action plan

Revisit Chapter 1 and consider the steps you can take to promote your own wellbeing. Consider taking time to complete the individual wellbeing action plan at the end of that chapter. Act as a role model to colleagues and students by sharing the process of writing a wellbeing action plan, or its elements, and encouraging others to do the same. Share the content of your wellbeing action plan with colleagues, friends or family and try to hold yourself to account for unashamedly prioritising your wellbeing. You could build on this idea by writing a wellbeing action plan for your whole department or school.

2. Take time to say 'thank you'

Begin regular staff meetings with a reflective gratitude list, keeping the focus on the positive. This is not only a great way to share the day-to-day successes of colleagues and students but can also set a very positive tone for the rest of your meeting. At first, it might be hard to decide what to share in these few moments at the start of a meeting, but before too long, everyone will become more attuned to keeping an eye out for reasons to be grateful to colleagues and there will be plenty to share.

3. Incorporate staff wellbeing into the roles of relevant senior staff

Consider whether there are any staff members who could oversee staff wellbeing as part of their remit. For example, this might make a natural addition to your mental health lead or designated mental health governor's role. Having senior members of staff championing wellbeing can ensure that it gets the airtime it deserves and does not fall off the agenda. A governor with a named responsibility for staff wellbeing can also ensure, as policies are developed or reviewed, that, where relevant, the impact on staff wellbeing is considered.

4. Build staff wellbeing measures into performance management procedures

When performance managing staff with line management responsibilities, create targets that pertain to the wellbeing of the staff they manage. In order to make this work you will also need to give them the time, space and potentially the budget needed to take steps to boost staff wellbeing.

5. Signpost support

Carry out an audit of support available to staff and ensure that this is well communicated; this might mean sharing it online and in poster form and regularly reminding staff during staff meetings. Consider the lines of support in school, locally and nationally, and consider both online and offline options.

Consider too how best to encourage a culture of help-seeking; there is little point in sharing support sources if colleagues are unwilling to engage. Again, senior leaders have a role to play here in recognising the importance of seeking help when needed, whether that's with lesson planning, mental health issues or anything else. A joint understanding between staff that seeking support is a sign of strength rather than weakness can help promote proactive help-seeking at a time when we're best able to engage, rather than waiting until we're completely overwhelmed.

Also consider whether staff can access support and guidance if they are due to teach a topic that is personally difficult for them due to their lived experience. We're good at thinking about how to safeguard students when teaching about sensitive issues like abuse and mental illness, but we can be less good at safeguarding staff.

6. How are you...actually?

Developing a culture of asking and answering the question 'How are you?' and actually meaning it is a small way to make a big difference. When we move beyond this question being a social tic and instead ask it when we have time to listen to a response, and we share a little of our ups and downs when asked, we create an environment where we're all a little more aware of how everyone is doing. We can celebrate each other's successes and support each other through wobbles.

7. Follow the five ways to wellbeing

Learn together about the 'Five ways to mental wellbeing' – an evidence-based approach to promoting wellbeing. The five ways are:

1. Connect

2. Be active

3. Take notice

4. Keep learning

5. Give

Each of the five ways is open to interpretation and there can be quite a lot of overlap. It's easy to find information and ideas online – think about small steps you could take and perhaps introduce the concept to students too.

More info here: www.gov.uk/government/publications/five-ways-to-mental-wellbeing.

8. Create a 'Shout Outs' board

In your staffroom, create a board where staff can share words of praise or thanks to celebrate the successes of colleagues, both within and beyond school. Remember to shout out to a range of colleagues, not just those who teach.

NOTES:

....

....

....

....

....

....

....

....

....

....

....

....

....

....

....

TRY THIS?

'We offer our student mental health worker for staff to see before and after school in confidence.' @iphonesrippin

IDEAS TO CHERRY PICK FROM

Each one of these ideas has worked for someone somewhere – take a look through the list and place a tick against any you think might be worth considering in your setting.

○ Run fitness classes

○ Provide a healthy lunch

○ Don't send emails out of hours

○ Have office staff acting as email gatekeepers

○ Share and learn from mistakes

○ Aim to reduce marking load

○ Review staff wellbeing regularly

○ Provide a wellbeing budget

○ Have regular socials

○ Perform random acts of kindness

○ Write thank you notes

○ Organise discounted gym memberships

○ Review meeting agendas to include wellbeing

○ Eat together

○ Find reasons to laugh

○ Organise a book club

○ Debrief staff who are handling distressing cases

○ Provide consistent communication mechanisms for all staff

○ Schedule 'open door' times for line managers so staff can pop in with any issues

○ Reduce the length of or number of staff meetings – for example, fortnightly instead of weekly

○ Have a feedback policy rather than a marking policy

○ Revamp the staffroom so that it is a calm space where colleagues can relax

○ Provide non-contact time for subject leaders

○ Allow staff to do PPA (planning, preparation and assessment) at home

○ Provide staff with free flu jabs

○ Introduce a buddy system for staff

○ Hold supportive, non-judgemental return-to-work meetings after absence

○ Have staff coffee once a week

○ Give staff access to coaching

INTRODUCING A MULTI-SCHOOL WELLBEING FORUM AT A SPECIAL SCHOOL IN STAFFORDSHIRE

Miranda Mellor is the staff wellbeing lead at a behaviour unit for 5–11-year-olds attached to a special school in Staffordshire. She writes about her role, working with a multi-academy trust (MAT)-wide wellbeing forum and the small steps that have a big impact on staff wellbeing.

One of the first tasks that the wellbeing leads from across the MAT took after being appointed was to identify issues and strengths using a wellbeing questionnaire and discussions with colleagues. This helped us to steer the senior leadership team towards some quick wins that would promote wellbeing and also meant we could share what was working well with other schools so we could learn from each other. I feel privileged to work in a team that helps each other. The small things that have a big impact on staff wellbeing that we identified in our unit included:

- Away days – once a year we have an inset day as a team away from work, doing something fun

- We all put £1 in for birthdays; a present and card are bought

- As our environment can be tough we have a daily debrief with the head of team so we are not taking worries home

- We have a team WhatsApp group

- We have a star of the week with fun prizes

Across the MAT, the wellbeing forum led on the organisation of a wellbeing day for all the children and staff at each school on the same day. During this time we focused our attention on the five ways to wellbeing: staying connected, being active, taking notice, learning and giving. Activities included: making stress balls, having hand massages, riding exercise bikes, yoga, taking photos, mindfulness.

Making this work for you

It was great to hear about Miranda's experience. There are a few things that stand out as important if you want to consider appointing a wellbeing lead in your school or developing a multi-school wellbeing forum:

- Appoint a lead who is passionate about wellbeing

  It's clear talking to Miranda that she really cares about the wellbeing of her colleagues and her students too; this makes her a fantastic champion for staff wellbeing, who's working hard to impact on school ethos and culture rather than simply ticking boxes or making tokenistic efforts.

- Ensure that there is senior leadership buy-in

Through the staff survey, colleagues shared ideas with Miranda about small changes they thought the senior leadership team could make to promote staff wellbeing. Senior leadership buy-in meant that these changes were relatively quick to implement, which sent a really positive message to all staff and was the beginning of a positive cycle of change for Miranda and colleagues.

- Share best practice across schools

Miranda works not just with her immediate colleagues in the unit she teaches in, but also with colleagues at the attached school and with colleagues across several schools who participated in the wellbeing forum. This means that best practice can easily be shared and that there is no need to constantly reinvent the wheel. Seeing your ideas replicated in neighbouring schools is also a great way of celebrating what's working well.

- Be willing to share challenges as well as successes

A culture of openness and honesty amongst the schools in the wellbeing forum meant that colleagues were also able to explore things that had had a negative impact on staff wellbeing in their school in the hope that other schools could learn from this too.

TRY THIS?

'We have given staff one wellbeing day to take at any point in the year.'
@sarahcombe

ACTION PLAN:
STAFF AT MY SCHOOL ARE HAPPY AND HEALTHY

	Short-term	**Medium-term**	**Long-term**
Baseline Score	Aim ☐	Aim ☐	Aim ☐
	Date ... / ... /	Date ... / ... /	Date ... / ... / ......
	Actual ☐	Actual ☐	Actual ☐
	Date ... / ... /	Date ... / ... /	Date ... / ... / ......

Set yourself a short-term, a medium-term and a longer-term aim of how you'd like to be scoring in this area. Be realistic and try to set achievable goals – you can always revise them up and down if you need to.

WHY DOES IT MATTER?

What are your motivations for working on this area – why does it matter to you and your school now? What difference might working on this area make?

....

....

....

....

....

....

CURRENT STRENGTHS

What is already working well and how can you build on this success?

....

....

....

....

....

....

CURRENT CHALLENGES

What is stopping you from scoring more highly here and how might you overcome these challenges?

....

....

....

....

....

....

....

AIM 1: A QUICK WIN – CHOOSE SOMETHING YOU CAN DO RIGHT AWAY TO MAKE A DIFFERENCE

....

....

....

....

....

....

....

WHY?

Why are you setting this aim?

....

....

....

....

....

....

....

WHO?
Who needs to be responsible, involved or persuaded?

. . . .

. . . .

. . . .

. . . .

. . . .

. . . .

. . . .

WHEN?
How long do you need to achieve this aim? How often should you review?

. . . .

. . . .

. . . .

. . . .

. . . .

. . . .

. . . .

HOW?
How will you achieve this aim – what actions need to be taken?

. . . .

. . . .

. . . .

. . . .

. . . .

. . . .

. . . .

WHAT?

What would success look like? What will be the impact? How will you measure it?

. . . .

. . . .

. . . .

. . . .

. . . .

. . . .

. . . .

REVIEW DATE: . . . .

REVIEW NOTES:

. . . .

. . . .

. . . .

. . . .

. . . .

. . . .

. . . .

. . . .

. . . .

. . . .

. . . .

. . . .

. . . .

AIM 2: A MEDIUM-TERM GOAL – WHAT CAN YOU AIM TO DO WITHIN THE NEXT THREE MONTHS?

....

....

....

....

....

....

....

WHY?

Why are you setting this aim?

....

....

....

....

....

....

....

WHO?

Who needs to be responsible, involved or persuaded?

....

....

....

....

....

....

....

WHEN?

How long do you need to achieve this aim? How often should you review?

. . . .

. . . .

. . . .

. . . .

. . . .

. . . .

. . . .

HOW?

How will you achieve this aim – what actions need to be taken?

. . . .

. . . .

. . . .

. . . .

. . . .

. . . .

. . . .

WHAT?

What would success look like? What will be the impact? How will you measure it?

. . . .

. . . .

. . . .

. . . .

. . . .

. . . .

. . . .

REVIEW DATE: . . . .

REVIEW NOTES:

. . . .

. . . .

. . . .

. . . .

. . . .

. . . .

. . . .

. . . .

. . . .

. . . .

. . . .

. . . .

. . . .

. . . .

. . . .

. . . .

. . . .

. . . .

. . . .

. . . .

. . . .

AIM 3: A LONGER-TERM CHALLENGE – WHAT IS GOING TO TAKE SIX MONTHS TO A YEAR TO ACHIEVE IF YOU START WORK ON IT RIGHT AWAY?

....

....

....

....

....

....

....

WHY?
Why are you setting this aim?

....

....

....

....

....

....

....

WHO?
Who needs to be responsible, involved or persuaded?

....

....

....

....

....

....

....

WHEN?

How long do you need to achieve this aim? How often should you review?

....

....

....

....

....

....

....

HOW?

How will you achieve this aim – what actions need to be taken?

....

....

....

....

....

....

....

WHAT?

What would success look like? What will be the impact? How will you measure it?

....

....

....

....

....

....

....

REVIEW DATE: . . . .

REVIEW NOTES:

. . . .

. . . .

. . . .

. . . .

. . . .

. . . .

. . . .

. . . .

. . . .

. . . .

. . . .

. . . .

. . . .

. . . .

. . . .

. . . .

. . . .

. . . .

. . . .

. . . .

. . . .

FURTHER READING

Live Well, Teach Well by Abigail Mann (London, 2018)

In this highly practical book, secondary school teacher Abigail explores 90 practical ideas for promoting the wellbeing of school staff. There's a really wide range of ideas – for example:

Idea 14: Wellbeing bags – wellbeing bags visibly lift the atmosphere in the staffroom.

Idea 42: Speedy lesson planning – understanding the basic elements of a lesson and sticking to them will keep things simple and save you time in the long run.

Idea 59: Beyond the classroom – extra-curricular activities develop positive relationships with students and promote wellbeing.

Chapter 4

MY SCHOOL FEELS SAFE AND WELCOMING

A safe and welcoming school is one in which students will thrive and flourish. They will feel able to be themselves and will know that their needs will be met; this will be true too of staff, parents and visitors. Walking into a school which feels warm and welcoming is enough to make any visitor walk with a bounce in their step; whilst a frosty welcome with angry shouting audible in the background is enough to set anyone on edge. Next time you walk through the doors to your school, imagine that you're visiting for the first time. Look around you – do the walls feel like people like you are welcome and valued here? Listen – can you hear a gentle hum of activity or can you hear sounds of anger or other loud noises that might make a sensitive child feel on edge? Do people say hello or smile and is there chaos in the corridors or a sense of order? How are people interacting with each other and is the school well signposted?

> 'I knew as soon as I walked in "I will be happy here" – the school had that special energy about it, buzzy, without being chaotic. Also, everyone was smiling – and it wasn't even Friday!'

Feeling safe is a basic human need

The need to feel safe is a fundamental human need that must be met if we are to flourish and learn. Where this need is not met, or perceived not to be met, it will be very difficult for learners to achieve as they could or should. For some learners, school may be the only place they feel safe; for these learners it is especially important that they feel welcomed when they arrive at school and they know that their basic right to feel safe will be met through the day. We can further meet this need to feel safe through creating a culture and environment that is predictable and consistent. Children feel safer when activities are rules bound and they know what to expect and what the consequences of their actions are.

When we create a safe, predictable environment in this way, we are creating the foundations from which children can not only engage but also can grow and flourish.

TRY THIS?

'My daughter's school has a therapy dog. The children can read to Kevin, particularly those receiving additional interventions. He's also involved in assemblies and treats. The children are going to be able to walk with him too.' @2yorkshiregirls

Impact on students, staff and parents

A school that feels warm and welcoming is one where not only students but also staff and parents will thrive. For many parents, school can be a place that holds difficult memories or it can feel otherwise intimidating; thinking about how to reach out to parents and making sure that when they do come into school they have a positive experience can have a big impact on their ability and willingness to engage and can help build bridges between the generations.

> 'I didn't have any happy memories of school and I've always considered myself to be a bit stupid, so I didn't like the idea of going in to my son's school – but it was actually OK. There were kids there to show us around, everything was clearly explained and it didn't feel anything like the horrible memories from my childhood.'

A warm and welcoming school can also create a sense of pride in students, parents and staff who can feel a real sense of belonging – another basic human need. No matter how diverse our student, staff and parent body, when we are all made to feel welcome and all feel proud to be associated with our school, we can feel like part of the same team – and that feels good!

TRY THIS?

'Our children are allowed and encouraged to talk to whichever adult they choose about things, it doesn't have to be their current class teacher.' @kazzannesturmey

EASING TRANSITION WITH STUDENT BEFRIENDERS IN THE NORTH OF ENGLAND

Cath Jackson is assistant head teacher at Kirkburton Middle School in a village in West Yorkshire, in the North of England. The school caters for children aged 10 to 14 and has 509 students.

Being a Befriender is a responsibility we introduced to the children in our school over 15 years ago. Befrienders are Year 8 (age 12 to 13) volunteers who are trained to be a peer support group and work closely with an adult Befriender. The group offers other children in school support with any concerns or worries they may have. Befrienders themselves develop inter-personal and social skills and help build self-esteem and emotional wellbeing in others.

Befrienders play a vital role in the transition work we do with our feeder schools. Transition activities take place fortnightly from January onwards, culminating in our new intake of students spending the whole of the last week of the summer term with us before they transfer the following autumn term. Befrienders are involved throughout this process. They are assigned to specific classes, play with the children at playtime, encourage new friendships, introduce new teachers, guide and help familiarise children with the school building and help them to understand the day-to-day running of our school. Befrienders spend valuable time welcoming our new children, getting to know them and taking them under their 'Befriender wings'.

Consequently our new children see the Befrienders as older peers they can turn to for guidance and support. Any fears they may have had about starting a new school are put to rest; they have made new friends, already know their teachers and feel safe, ready to start the new year positively with few or no worries over the summer holidays.

TRY THIS?

'Ravenstone Primary School focuses on several core values, e.g. kindness, and these have been adopted into school culture and are consistently praised using various strategies, e.g. daily values postcards, and referenced to if behaviour is inconsistent with values rather than having a dominant focus on rules.' @bye_amanda

COLLECTING IDEAS:
MY SCHOOL FEELS SAFE AND WELCOMING

This space is for you to jot down your thoughts and ideas as they arise. I've split it into start, stop, continue and change, which can be a neat way of thinking about the actions we need to take. You might make a few notes of things you learned during the Mentally Healthy School Audit/Go Out And Listen exercise (see the end of Chapter 2) or you could make notes of your ideas as you read this chapter. Revisit this space and keep track of additional ideas as they arise here. It's not meant to be perfect or beautiful, it's just a place to keep your ideas so you can refer to it when you do your action planning.

Things to START doing…

. . . .

. . . .

. . . .

. . . .

. . . .

. . . .

. . . .

. . . .

. . . .

Things to STOP doing…

. . . .

. . . .

. . . .

. . . .

. . . .

. . . .

. . . .

. . . .

. . . .

Things to CONTINUE doing…

. . . .

. . . .

. . . .

. . . .

. . . .

. . . .

. . . .

. . . .

Things to CHANGE our way of doing…

. . . .

. . . .

. . . .

. . . .

. . . .

. . . .

. . . .

. . . .

Other notes:

. . . .

. . . .

. . . .

. . . .

. . . .

. . . .

EIGHT PRACTICAL STEPS YOU COULD TAKE

The key is not to take all of these steps, but rather to identify a few that feel like a good fit and to focus on how you might go about achieving those. Use the action plan later in this chapter to help you.

1. Think about the 'visitor journey'

Step into the shoes of someone visiting your school for the first time, or better still ask a friend or colleague to act as a mystery shopper. Think about the process of arriving at the school and how clear and welcoming this is. Simple things like clear signage about where to go and what is expected can make a huge difference to how a visitor is feeling by the time they are sitting in the reception area.

2. Welcome everybody consistently

Friendly frontline staff can make all visitors feel well looked after very quickly by doing simple things like acknowledging people as they arrive; clearly talking them through any sign-in or safeguarding processes; and offering a drink or taking away dripping coats and umbrellas. Treating both adults and children well as they arrive at the school, especially for the first time, can really have an impact. Reception areas where a range of student work is displayed (that is less than a decade old!) or where thought has been taken about something you might look at or read whilst waiting always feel especially welcoming.

3. Create positive signage that explains policies

In order to keep everybody safe, there are lots of rules in schools – think about how these rules are displayed and how they might be interpreted by a visitor. For example, many schools have a no phones policy – instead of a big 'No Phones' sign, a sign which politely asks for phones to remain in bags or which gives a little explanation as to why phones shouldn't be used can feel less off-putting. Alternatively, you can have important policies like these briefly explained in person by frontline staff. There are many such policies and procedures in school that we all take for granted, but a visitor might easily fall foul of one of these and end up feeling like they're being told off if they get things wrong.

4. Hello and a smile

As well as having frontline staff who are warm and welcoming, consider too how staff and students greet visitors around the school. Being greeted with a hello and a smile can make a big scary school feel less daunting when we visit for the first time. Hellos and smiles can be given and received by children and adults alike.

5. Clear, consistently enforced rules

An important way of enabling students to feel safe is to have clear, consistently followed rules so that they know what is expected of them and the consequences of their behaviour. Sometimes, we feel we are doing a kindness by bending the rules for a child in need; but in general children feel safest and thrive best when their environment is predictable. If you do have to change the rules, discuss the new parameters and expectations with the child concerned and be consistent in applying the adapted rules.

6. Meet and greet every learner

Taking a moment to greet every learner by name as they arrive at class gives each child a moment of connection, helps them to feel a sense of belonging and helps to ready them for learning.

7. Represent diversity of learners and learning in displays

Our school displays can have a big impact on boosting the self-esteem of our learners and can send strong messages about what kind of school we are. Think about whether the images shared around your school represent the diversity of your school community and whether there are any students who might not see people like themselves mirrored in the school's displays. Think too about how you can celebrate every kind of success in the displays you develop. Think both in terms of looking beyond academic work to think about how to celebrate other endeavours and also about how you can celebrate effort as well as attainment. Whether or not we intend them to, our school displays are one of the key ways we communicate our beliefs about our schools and our expectations of and hopes for our students. Stop to consider what story your displays are telling and whether there are any students who might feel excluded from that story.

8. Create calm spaces

Does your school have calm, quiet spaces that students can visit if they're feeling overwhelmed or if they simply want a little quiet time? The school environment is often buzzy and busy and this can be a lot for anyone to manage hour after hour, especially for students who have special or additional needs. Breaktimes and lunchtimes can be especially tricky; is there somewhere that students can go if they would like to be warm or calm? Book corners or libraries are often a good starting point.

NOTES:

. . . .

. . . .

. . . .

. . . .

. . . .

. . . .

. . . .

. . . .

. . . .

. . . .

. . . .

. . . .

. . . .

. . . .

TRY THIS?

'Ensure that parents think of the whole school community whilst on school grounds – being polite, respectful to others and being good role models. Loud, intimidating and foul-mouthed parents create fear in the children and other parents and should be dealt with swiftly by staff.' @annatwis

CREATING A SENSE OF COMMUNITY WITH A BRIGHT BLUE UNIFORM IN BRISTOL

Julia Skinner, an ex-head teacher from Bristol, explains how a school uniform helped to create a sense of community amongst staff and parents following a school amalgamation.

When I opened the new school which was an amalgamation of my junior school with our feeder infant school, parents were not happy about it. The schools, although geographically very near, did not work closely together, so when the local authority announced its intention to amalgamate the two, it was no surprise that the infant school parents were unhappy about their school closing and their children moving to the 'big' school.

The new primary of 450 children was in South Bristol in a centre of social deprivation with many children coming from 'workless homes' where for generations getting a job was hard if not impossible and school was a place where children should be happy before learning. I was appointed head designate of the primary a year before it opened. Although that meant setting up a new school whilst running the junior school, it did give me and the staff time to get to know the community and share our ideas for the new school.

I would regularly go to the infant building to meet with staff and parents. Sometimes this was a formal session with a specific question-and-answer opportunity. At other times it was more social with tea and cakes. I remember my first parents' 'surgery' where a parent folded her arms and said in a loud voice 'I don't know why they've got to go over THERE. Those big ones will bully them. They'll get lost.' I knew I had my work cut out.

To help the amalgamation, the local authority provided a new school jumper for every child. We chose a colour that was available from most supermarkets but their first had the newly designed logo on it. The new school was opening at a time when many secondaries in the city were becoming academies and joining trusts and they all seemed to provide a free blazer. I don't know if the uniform provider had delusions of grandeur but we had the usual array of uniform available and also coats.

The coats were full length, waterproof outers with fleece inners and were very popular. I wasn't sure that they would sell but they certainly did – to the point of having a waiting list for new ones to come in. The biggest surprise though was a request from parents to have them for themselves! The supplier was obviously taken aback as he really had to work out how his company could organise 'big' coats, but he did, and, before long, across the district you could spot the bright blue of the new school.

I was SO proud of these parents, walking around the area with MY uniform on. Oh, and remember the outspoken parent? She became my chair of governors in our second year. A definite huge tick for parents engaging positively, I think!

IDEAS TO CHERRY PICK FROM

Each one of these ideas has worked for someone somewhere – take a look through the list and place a tick against any you think might be worth considering in your setting.

- ○ Create student-friendly versions of policies and procedures
- ○ Greet students with their choice of handshake, high five or hug
- ○ Meet and greet everyone kindly
- ○ Be inquisitive, not punitive, regarding lateness
- ○ Update displays to make them feel inclusive
- ○ Think about what story your website tells about your school
- ○ Aim for calm but happy 'buzz'
- ○ Have expectations of leaders as well as learners
- ○ Have a range of spaces for use at break
- ○ Have zero tolerance of bullying
- ○ Support those who bully as well as those who are bullied
- ○ Have buddy benches/peer supporters
- ○ Employ a school counsellor
- ○ Colour-code visitor lanyards to denote safeguarding level
- ○ Name staff who can support with specific issues, for example LGBTQ+
- ○ Have older buddies or peer mentors who've been through it before
- ○ Ensure everyone has someone they can talk to
- ○ Give rewards for trying hard, not just scoring highly
- ○ Consider how not to penalise children with disability or chronic illness when rewarding attendance with parties or treats
- ○ Educate openly about neurodiversity and mental health
- ○ Support an 'it's OK not to be OK' culture
- ○ Understand sensory needs and offer adaptions for these
- ○ Value all children's strengths and differences; see what a child can do, rather than focusing on what they can't
- ○ Listen to students and be honest with them, even if it means disappointing them
- ○ Train all staff in active listening to enable students to talk to whichever adult they feel most comfortable with if they have an issue
- ○ Consider how adults interact with each other as well as how they interact with children; students learn a lot from seeing adults greeting one another kindly

ACTION PLAN:
MY SCHOOL FEELS SAFE AND WELCOMING

	Short-term	Medium-term	Long-term
Baseline Score	Aim ☐	Aim ☐	Aim ☐
	Date .../.../.......	Date .../.../.......	Date .../.../.......
	Actual ☐	Actual ☐	Actual ☐
	Date.../.../.......	Date.../.../.......	Date.../.../.......

Set yourself a short-term, a medium-term and a longer-term aim of how you'd like to be scoring in this area. Be realistic and try to set achievable goals – you can always revise them up and down if you need to.

WHY DOES IT MATTER?

What are your motivations for working on this area – why does it matter to you and your school now? What difference might working on this area make?

. . . .

. . . .

. . . .

. . . .

. . . .

. . . .

CURRENT STRENGTHS

What is already working well and how can you build on this success?

. . . .

. . . .

. . . .

. . . .

. . . .

. . . .

CURRENT CHALLENGES

What is stopping you from scoring more highly here and how might you overcome these challenges?

....

....

....

....

....

....

....

AIM 1: A QUICK WIN – CHOOSE SOMETHING YOU CAN DO RIGHT AWAY TO MAKE A DIFFERENCE

....

....

....

....

....

....

....

WHY?

Why are you setting this aim?

....

....

....

....

....

....

WHO?
Who needs to be responsible, involved or persuaded?

. . . .

. . . .

. . . .

. . . .

. . . .

. . . .

. . . .

WHEN?
How long do you need to achieve this aim? How often should you review?

. . . .

. . . .

. . . .

. . . .

. . . .

. . . .

. . . .

HOW?
How will you achieve this aim – what actions need to be taken?

. . . .

. . . .

. . . .

. . . .

. . . .

. . . .

. . . .

WHAT?
What would success look like? What will be the impact? How will you measure it?

....

....

....

....

....

....

....

REVIEW DATE: ....

REVIEW NOTES:

....

....

....

....

....

....

....

....

....

....

....

....

....

....

....

....

AIM 2: A MEDIUM-TERM GOAL – WHAT CAN YOU AIM TO DO WITHIN THE NEXT THREE MONTHS?

....

....

....

....

....

....

....

WHY?
Why are you setting this aim?

....

....

....

....

....

....

....

WHO?
Who needs to be responsible, involved or persuaded?

....

....

....

....

....

....

....

WHEN?

How long do you need to achieve this aim? How often should you review?

. . . .

. . . .

. . . .

. . . .

. . . .

. . . .

. . . .

HOW?

How will you achieve this aim – what actions need to be taken?

. . . .

. . . .

. . . .

. . . .

. . . .

. . . .

. . . .

WHAT?

What would success look like? What will be the impact? How will you measure it?

. . . .

. . . .

. . . .

. . . .

. . . .

. . . .

REVIEW DATE: . . . .

REVIEW NOTES:

. . . .

. . . .

. . . .

. . . .

. . . .

. . . .

. . . .

. . . .

. . . .

. . . .

. . . .

. . . .

. . . .

. . . .

. . . .

. . . .

. . . .

. . . .

. . . .

. . . .

. . . .

AIM 3: A LONGER-TERM CHALLENGE – WHAT IS GOING TO TAKE SIX MONTHS TO A YEAR TO ACHIEVE IF YOU START WORK ON IT RIGHT AWAY?

....
....
....
....
....
....
....

WHY?
Why are you setting this aim?

....
....
....
....
....
....
....

WHO?
Who needs to be responsible, involved or persuaded?

....
....
....
....
....
....
....

WHEN?

How long do you need to achieve this aim? How often should you review?

. . . .

. . . .

. . . .

. . . .

. . . .

. . . .

. . . .

HOW?

How will you achieve this aim – what actions need to be taken?

. . . .

. . . .

. . . .

. . . .

. . . .

. . . .

. . . .

WHAT?

What would success look like? What will be the impact? How will you measure it?

. . . .

. . . .

. . . .

. . . .

. . . .

. . . .

REVIEW DATE: . . . .

REVIEW NOTES:

. . . .

. . . .

. . . .

. . . .

. . . .

. . . .

. . . .

. . . .

. . . .

. . . .

. . . .

. . . .

. . . .

. . . .

. . . .

. . . .

. . . .

. . . .

. . . .

. . . .

CREATING SAFE SPACES FOR VULNERABLE LEARNERS

Clare Erasmus, a wellbeing lead and teacher with 20 years' experience, shares her ideas for creating safe spaces for vulnerable learners. This is an abridged version of an article that was first shared in the *TES* magazine and online at www.tes.com.

A safe space in school is one where a young person has some control over what happens next; where, for a few moments, they can press 'pause' and gather their emotions; somewhere they feel less threatened and overwhelmed by what is happening; a place where, if they want to talk to someone without fear of being judged or exposed, they can.

What should this look like?

I believe pop-up safe spaces can easily operate at lunch, in classrooms, using trained peers and teaching staff. They should have a range of purposes depending on the needs in your school community. Here are a few suggestions I have seen trialled out effectively in my 20 years of teaching.

The anti-bullying room

This is where students can come and talk about experiences of bullying or even just a breakdown in friendship communication. Reports can be filed and investigated by staff, and day-to-day peer mentoring and signposting can take place by trained anti-bullying mentors from the student body. Restorative sessions can take place here, too.

The wellbeing room

This is where students can come to talk about personal issues that they are facing with a trained 'wellbeing ambassador', who will listen without judgement and signpost support in and outside of the school. This is an effective space to direct a young person to if they are facing complex mental wellbeing challenges that could be a safeguarding concern – as long as staff or ambassadors manning the room are trained in the school's safeguarding procedure.

The 'Q' zone

This is where students who are feeling anxious or vulnerable can go – often it will be students who find the business of secondary school social life all too much and they can quietly sit here and chill out. Access to this space should be by invitation or referral-only from staff and peer mentors, keeping it as safe as possible. Various calming activities can take place here, from mindfulness colouring-in, journal writing, chess and board games to playing Minecraft in 'creative' mode. Often, this space will be inhabited by young people on the autistic spectrum.

The gay/straight alliance space

In our school, this was a student-led movement where the goal was to make the school community safe by challenging homophobia and homophobic language. This can be a great space for breaking down barriers and encouraging a school community to become more supportive, while also creating a culture of respect, so students can feel safe and free to concentrate at school.

The young carers' space

This is where young carers can gather, get support from staff and find solidarity with other young carers as they cope with the demands of their caring responsibilities. Sometimes a sympathetic or supportive chat can make a huge difference to the young carer. Sometimes they don't need to chat; they just need a simple acknowledgement that they are doing an amazing job. It also enables schools to be more vigilant and help track the wellbeing of their young carers and spot any warning signs or concerning trends.

The Year 7-only playground

This is a safe space for the transition year as the young 11- and 12-year-olds find their feet and confidence at secondary school. Here, they can feel free to continue with their Year 6 'play' mindset without fear of ridicule from the older students.

These are just suggestions: you should assess the needs of your student body and respond accordingly, pulling in volunteers and external agencies where appropriate, but also giving power to students where possible.

Making it work in your school

I have found it extremely useful to take an area of the school, ideally a corridor of classrooms, and name it the wellbeing zone for the lunch period, arranging the pop-ups in each classroom in that area.

The location of the wellbeing zone matters. It is important that it is seen as something separate from the special educational needs and disability space because we need to recognise that having a mental wellbeing challenge does not always equate with a learning need. It needs to be destigmatised in schools and given its own signposting and space. Otherwise many of the young people who are facing challenges won't visit as they don't see themselves as having a learning need.

These rooms need to be consistently open every lunchtime, with a trained staff member and peers in the rooms ready to listen and support.

What is vital is that these spaces deliver on their promise. If this consistency can be achieved, the reputation and trust of these rooms and the people in them will be gained and the young people will use them.

FURTHER READING

How to Create Kind Schools by Jenny Hulme (London, 2015)

In this book, Jenny explores a range of projects being used by schools to create a happy environment where every child feels included. The initiatives she explores include dance workshops, gardening clubs, autism ambassadors, gay role models, peer mentoring schemes and traveller community theatre productions. I love this book as it's full of inspiration and outside-of-the-box thinking, but also shows the little ways in which schools can make a big difference and create kind and cohesive communities.

Chapter 5

THE VOICE OF EVERY LEARNER IS HEARD AND VALUED

In recent years, schools have grown a lot better at engaging with student voice, and this is reflected in the curriculum, policies and procedures which can be best tailored to meet the needs of our current students, when we listen to what they have to say. It's important though that we ensure that every voice is heard, not just the louder ones, as there can be a tendency for a vocal minority to have their voices heard above the voices of their peers.

The expert on the student is the student

When we find ways to ensure we go beyond tokenistic gestures and genuinely listen to what our students have to say, and act on this appropriately, we put ourselves in the best possible position to create an environment and culture where our students can enjoy and achieve. Arguably, there is no one who can better tell us the needs of our students than the students themselves. This is an ongoing process as students' experiences and needs are constantly evolving, so we need not just to listen once, but to keep on listening.

TRY THIS?

'Have opportunities for students to answer the statement: "I wish my teacher knew..."' @4heartsandminds

Some voices dominate

There will always be a minority of students who are more able than their peers to make their voices heard. We need to be careful not to assume that engaging with these students alone is enough. Their opinions and experiences are important and valid, but they are not representative of our entire student population. It's important in particular to ensure that we engage with students representing vulnerable groups – especially when we're considering issues related to mental health and wellbeing.

Some voices are easily lost

In order to ensure that every voice is heard and valued, we need to pay special attention to those students who might ordinarily fly under the radar – the quiet child who floats by without any extremes of behaviour, who gives no cause for concern and rarely raises their head above the parapet. These are the students whose voice is most likely to get lost, but their experiences are valid too, so finding ways to engage with these students is important if we're to understand the full picture.

TRY THIS?

'Ask parents if they will write you a letter telling you the things about their child you would never otherwise find out (e.g. scared of spiders, close to grandma).' @sue_cowley

NOTES:

....

....

....

....

....

....

....

....

....

....

....

....

....

....

COLLECTING IDEAS:
THE VOICE OF EVERY LEARNER
IS HEARD AND VALUED

This space is for you to jot down your thoughts and ideas as they arise. I've split it into start, stop, continue and change, which can be a neat way of thinking about the actions we need to take. You might make a few notes of things you learned during the Mentally Healthy School Audit/Go Out And Listen exercise (see the end of Chapter 2) or you could make notes of your ideas as you read this chapter. Revisit this space and keep track of additional ideas as they arise here. It's not meant to be perfect or beautiful, it's just a place to keep your ideas so you can refer to it when you do your action planning.

Things to START doing…

....

....

....

....

....

....

....

....

Things to STOP doing…

....

....

....

....

....

....

....

....

Things to CONTINUE doing...

. . . .

. . . .

. . . .

. . . .

. . . .

. . . .

. . . .

. . . .

Things to CHANGE our way of doing...

. . . .

. . . .

. . . .

. . . .

. . . .

. . . .

. . . .

. . . .

Other notes:

. . . .

. . . .

. . . .

. . . .

. . . .

. . . .

EIGHT PRACTICAL STEPS YOU COULD TAKE

The key is not to take all of these steps, but rather to identify a few that feel like a good fit and to focus on how you might go about achieving those. Use the action plan later in this chapter to help you.

1. Invite governors to be a student for the day

Governors make a lot of important decisions about school, but they often meet after hours and rarely get a chance to interact with students (or staff) unless they are a parent or staff governor. Inviting your governors to join the school as a student for the day can help them to see things from a student's perspective. Pair each governor with a student or two and have them shadow that student throughout the day. Brief students beforehand and encourage them to carry on their day as normally as possible and encourage them to share their thoughts, ideas and experiences with visiting governors. It works best if the whole governing body (including staff governors) are able to participate so they can be paired with a range of students and then report back to share what they've learned.

2. Include students in your leadership teams

Consider how you might best engage student voice at middle and senior leadership levels. You will not want to engage students with every aspect of management and leadership, but there will be some areas where student input is especially welcomed. Consider whether students could be involved in parts of meetings, either to present their ideas and answer questions, or as a genuine part of the team discussing the issues in hand.

3. Carry out student surveys

A good way to get a quick overview of student experiences and ideas is to survey the student body. Developing a means for collecting data in this way can provide an opportunity for even the quietest voices to be heard, and if you repeat the exercise at regular intervals, it can also be a good way to check progress over time.

If you'd like to carry out student surveys related to wellbeing but aren't sure where to start, the Anna Freud Centre's wellbeing measurement toolkit is a great place to start. It explores a wide range of measurement tools and surveys and will help you to determine what will be the best fit for your school. You can access it at: www.annafreud.org/what-we-do/schools-in-mind/resources-for-schools/mental-health-toolkit-for-schools.

4. Have anonymous ideas boxes

Allowing students to share their ideas anonymously can increase the likelihood of them sharing honest feedback, thoughts and ideas. This can be done simply through anonymous question or ideas boxes either physically placed in the building or provided online. If you'd like students to be able to remain genuinely anonymous when sharing in this way, think about how to protect anonymity. For example, an ideas box that is placed in an overlooked reception area might make students less likely to participate than a box sitting in a quiet corner somewhere. Similarly, if a student has to share an email address or class details to log an idea online, this might hinder honest sharing.

5. Have a 'You asked, we did' board

If your school is working hard to listen to what students want and to respond appropriately, then this is worth shouting about! Celebrating the changes that have come about as a result of student suggestions via a physical or online noticeboard is a great reminder to students that their opinion matters.

6. Involve students in the development and delivery of PSHE education

For some areas of PSHE (Personal, Social, Health and Economic Education) it can be incredibly powerful to involve older students in the development and delivery of lessons as they will have a clear understanding of what younger students are going through and what might genuinely help. Sometimes students are more likely to listen to older peers than to a teacher as they feel that their peers 'get them' – this can be powerful both for the young people teaching and those learning. Of course, you must take care to support students in the preparation and delivery of lessons, especially if this touches on sensitive issues, but with due care taken this can be incredibly powerful for all concerned.

7. Sit and eat with students

Taking time to chat with students informally over lunch can be an incredibly effective way to increase our understanding of what matters to them, how things are going and what they need support with. Whilst holding focus groups or sending out surveys can be valuable, being part of day-to-day conversations with students gives us a far deeper insight into their lives. It's also a great way for us to get to know our students better and sends a strong message to them that they are valued. Of course, we can't all do this every day, but taking a little time to chew the cud with your students now and then can be time incredibly well spent.

8. Collaborate with other schools

If you have a student council, peer mentors or peer educators, consider whether they would benefit from collaborating with their equivalent in other schools. Often, there is much to be learnt from students having their horizons broadened by working with peers from other schools. It can often help them appreciate what is good about their school and what could be better too. It can also help both students and staff come up with new ideas for engaging the voice of every learner.

NOTES:

. . . .

. . . .

. . . .

. . . .

. . . .

. . . .

. . . .

. . . .

. . . .

. . . .

. . . .

. . . .

. . . .

. . . .

. . . .

. . . .

. . . .

THE 'CHANGE YOUR MIND' SCHEME AT QUEEN MARY'S IN WALSALL

Sophie McPhee, the PSHE coordinator at Queen Mary's Grammar School in Walsall, talked to me about the powerful 'Change Your Mind' scheme that her students have been engaging with. Queen Mary's Grammar School is a selective 11–18 boys' school, co-educational in the sixth form, drawing students from a wide range of socio-economic and ethnic backgrounds, and is a founder member of the Mercian Trust, currently comprising five Walsall secondary schools.

Our 'Change Your Mind' scheme, now in its third year, started with four Year 12 students (16–17-year-olds) from the School Council who wanted to plan and run a mental health project with my support. They intended to submit the project to the national Speaker's School Council Competition and wanted to contribute to the whole-school drive to improve mental health provision at Queen Mary's, launched in 2016 by Richard Langton, who is now headmaster.

A couple of months later, these students visited six primary schools, delivering workshops they had planned on either 'Digital Detoxing' or 'Transition to Secondary School' to Year 6 (10–11-year-olds), and when they eventually submitted their project to the competition, they were awarded the runners-up prize in their age category.

One student in particular from this team, Pavandeep Josan, was passionate about continuing the project the following academic year despite the competition having come to an end. He set about expanding the team and, in its second year, around 25 17- and 18-year-olds went out to 14 primary schools, leading to the project being Highly Commended in the Mayor of Walsall's Community and Excellence Awards 2018.

Now the scheme is in its third year, and due to its success, it has evolved again to become a curriculum option for Year 12. I have written a programme of weekly lessons whereby the students plan and deliver presentations to one another on a diverse range of PSHE themes, all of which are linked directly or indirectly to mental health, such as fake news, autism, nutrition and living an enriching life. A draft version of the programme was discussed and amended in a meeting with Pavandeep and the rest of our Student Senior Leadership Team last summer, ahead of being launched in September.

The current team is now getting ready to visit the 20 primary schools who have already signed up this year, including several who will be receiving their second or third visit. We are due to reach over 900 10- and 11-year-olds in Walsall already, but are aiming for 1000 by the end of the school year. One of the strengths of the current programme is that the Year 12 students give written feedback to one another, leading to the awarding of a bronze, silver or gold 'Change Your Mind' logo badge and certificate at the end of the year, and an evidence folder which can be presented at interviews for universities, apprenticeships or jobs.

Making it work in your school

For those wishing to set up a similar scheme in their school, it can be done at very little cost. We have expanded our number of schools largely due to advertising the project via email and Twitter, and if you didn't want to go to the expense of providing each primary student with a logo sticker as we are doing, or awarding the sixth-formers badges and certificates, the only cost would be the photocopying of lesson materials. The scheme is beneficial to all parties involved: both Year 6 and Year 12 students enhance their understanding of how to maintain optimum mental health, whilst at the same time the older students develop their soft skills, and links between schools in the local community are strengthened.

TRY THIS?

'We recommend schools consult with students on strategic matters important to them: e.g. asking young carers what should be in the young carers policy.' The Children's Society

NOTES:

. . . .

. . . .

. . . .

. . . .

. . . .

. . . .

. . . .

. . . .

. . . .

. . . .

. . . .

. . . .

. . . .

IDEAS TO CHERRY PICK FROM

Each one of these ideas has worked for someone somewhere – take a look through the list and place a tick against any you think might be worth considering in your setting.

- Have a school council or student voice ambassadors

- Involve students in senior leadership team meetings

- Hold surveys or focus groups

- Have 'ask it baskets' or worry monsters

- Explore and celebrate difference in assemblies, displays and in class

- Consider incorporating student voice into staff appraisals

- Hold student drop-in sessions

- Encourage school leaders to lunch with students

- Involve students in staff recruitment

- Make sure student leadership positions within the school such as school council/head girl, etc. are representative of the diversity of the school, not just those who are confident

- Involve students in developing and enforcing school rules and policies

- Don't over-focus on data – remember the young person is at the centre

- Introduce an ideas scheme where students can submit ideas for improvements at school and any ideas taken forward will be rewarded or recognised

- Appoint student and staff wellbeing champions to promote wellbeing

- Create safe environments for shy children to reflect on their learning and feel heard

- Where students don't have the ability to communicate their needs/wants verbally, find other strategies to show that their opinions matter too and allow them to be involved

- Encourage positive remarks between peers using a 'See it, say it' approach

- Learn to listen calmly in moments of challenging behaviour

- Appoint a link governor to attend the school's student council

ACTION PLAN:
THE VOICE OF EVERY LEARNER IS HEARD AND VALUED

	Short-term	**Medium-term**	**Long-term**
Baseline Score	Aim ☐	Aim ☐	Aim ☐
	Date .../.../.......	Date .../.../.......	Date .../.../.......
	Actual ☐	Actual ☐	Actual ☐
	Date .../.../.......	Date .../.../.......	Date .../.../.......

Set yourself a short-term, a medium-term and a longer-term aim of how you'd like to be scoring in this area. Be realistic and try to set achievable goals – you can always revise them up and down if you need to.

WHY DOES IT MATTER?

What are your motivations for working on this area – why does it matter to you and your school now? What difference might working on this area make?

....
....
....
....
....
....

CURRENT STRENGTHS

What is already working well and how can you build on this success?

....
....
....
....
....

CURRENT CHALLENGES

What is stopping you from scoring more highly here and how might you overcome these challenges?

. . . .

. . . .

. . . .

. . . .

. . . .

. . . .

. . . .

AIM 1: A QUICK WIN - CHOOSE SOMETHING YOU CAN DO RIGHT AWAY TO MAKE A DIFFERENCE

. . . .

. . . .

. . . .

. . . .

. . . .

. . . .

. . . .

WHY?

Why are you setting this aim?

. . . .

. . . .

. . . .

. . . .

. . . .

. . . .

WHO?
Who needs to be responsible, involved or persuaded?

. . . .

. . . .

. . . .

. . . .

. . . .

. . . .

. . . .

WHEN?
How long do you need to achieve this aim? How often should you review?

. . . .

. . . .

. . . .

. . . .

. . . .

. . . .

. . . .

HOW?
How will you achieve this aim – what actions need to be taken?

. . . .

. . . .

. . . .

. . . .

. . . .

. . . .

WHAT?

What would success look like? What will be the impact? How will you measure it?

. . . .
. . . .
. . . .
. . . .
. . . .
. . . .
. . . .

REVIEW DATE: . . . .

REVIEW NOTES:

. . . .
. . . .
. . . .
. . . .
. . . .
. . . .
. . . .
. . . .
. . . .
. . . .
. . . .
. . . .
. . . .
. . . .
WHAT? . . . .

AIM 2: A MEDIUM-TERM GOAL – WHAT CAN YOU AIM TO DO WITHIN THE NEXT THREE MONTHS?

....

....

....

....

....

....

....

WHY?
Why are you setting this aim?

....

....

....

....

....

....

....

WHO?
Who needs to be responsible, involved or persuaded?

....

....

....

....

....

....

WHEN?

How long do you need to achieve this aim? How often should you review?

....

....

....

....

....

....

....

HOW?

How will you achieve this aim – what actions need to be taken?

....

....

....

....

....

....

....

WHAT?

What would success look like? What will be the impact? How will you measure it?

....

....

....

....

....

....

....

REVIEW DATE: . . . .

REVIEW NOTES:

. . . .

. . . .

. . . .

. . . .

. . . .

. . . .

. . . .

. . . .

. . . .

. . . .

. . . .

. . . .

. . . .

. . . .

. . . .

. . . .

. . . .

. . . .

. . . .

. . . .

. . . .

. . . .

AIM 3: A LONGER-TERM CHALLENGE – WHAT IS GOING TO TAKE SIX MONTHS TO A YEAR TO ACHIEVE IF YOU START WORK ON IT RIGHT AWAY?

....

....

....

....

....

....

....

WHY?
Why are you setting this aim?

....

....

....

....

....

....

....

WHO?
Who needs to be responsible, involved or persuaded?

....

....

....

....

....

....

....

WHEN?

How long do you need to achieve this aim? How often should you review?

. . . .

. . . .

. . . .

. . . .

. . . .

. . . .

. . . .

HOW?

How will you achieve this aim – what actions need to be taken?

. . . .

. . . .

. . . .

. . . .

. . . .

. . . .

. . . .

WHAT?

What would success look like? What will be the impact? How will you measure it?

. . . .

. . . .

. . . .

. . . .

. . . .

. . . .

REVIEW DATE: . . . .

REVIEW NOTES:

. . . .

. . . .

. . . .

. . . .

. . . .

. . . .

. . . .

. . . .

. . . .

. . . .

. . . .

. . . .

. . . .

. . . .

. . . .

. . . .

. . . .

. . . .

. . . .

. . . .

. . . .

TRY THIS?

'Have sticky notes handy so the children can comment: "What did you enjoy?" "What didn't you like?" "What did you learn?" It can be a sentence or just a one-word answer.' @pixtink

IMPLEMENTING A PEER LISTENING SCHEME AT A CO-EDUCATIONAL SCHOOL IN LONDON

Sharon Goldstone, deputy safeguarding lead and mental health and wellbeing officer at Chingford Foundation School, told me about the evolution and impact of her school's peer listening scheme. Chingford Foundation School is a co-educational academy with sixth form based in North East London in the Borough of Waltham Forest.

With many young people under increased pressures and being identified with mental health issues and fewer outside agency interventions available due to funding cuts, we had to find ways of doing things differently, which enabled young people to access support before problems escalated.

To respond to this dilemma, I established a new school provision, with a focus on the more vulnerable students incorporating: a Safeguarding First Line Assessment Service and a Mental Health and Wellbeing First Aid Triage Service.

Through close working with local CAMHS (Child and Adolescent Mental Health Services) professionals we are more adept at recognising early warning signs and distinguishing nuanced behaviours through an approachable, accessible and collaborative service.

Past service users were keen to support each other, so we set up a peer listening scheme: a less threatening pop-up wellbeing zone, a place for those experiencing difficulties to pause, gather thoughts and speak to a team of trained peer listeners about issues of concern.

Peer listeners from all age ranges were recruited and completed a two-day training programme along with some staff supporters, based on issues including: empathy, active listening, verbal and non-verbal communication, confidentiality and problem solving. They operate a rota and are present in the playground wearing bright badges and vests, offering private conversations or making appointments through a self-referral form. Peer listeners are supported through weekly sharing circles, where cases are discussed anonymously, and further training provided.

Since the scheme started, valuable support has been provided to students, with real opportunities for peer listeners to develop skills and confidence. The school sees this as a very visible way of showing that they are encouraging students to talk about their feelings and that the student voice is heard.

The peer listening scheme was commended by Ofsted and included in the practice examples of the Healthy London Partnership Mental Health in Schools Toolkit.

Running the scheme requires a significant investment of time and a committed project coordinator who can influence and persuade, is willing to learn from others and yet can take a strong lead in managing the service. But it's hugely worthwhile, having a measurable impact on those using the service, the peer listeners and the school's ethos and culture.

TRY THIS?

'We have a display showing the school council members and the agendas of their meetings as well as a notice board near the school entrance with things that parents and students have asked for, and the school's response.' @jennyhillparker

FURTHER READING

Essential Listening Skills for Busy School Staff by Nick Luxmoore (London, 2014)

This is one of my favourite books to recommend and I gift copies of it to many of the schools I work with. It's a slim book but packed full of down-to-earth ideas to help school staff provide quality listening to students. It helps us realise the big impact we can have in a small amount of time and gives highly practical pointers for doing so. The author, Nick, has a wide range of experience and is both a trained teacher and counsellor, which makes him uniquely well placed to advise on how to listen well at school. He also draws on a variety of first-hand experiences outlining conversations that went well, and learning from those that went less well, and he provides specific tips for listening in a range of situations that school staff may worry about finding themselves dealing with – for example, supporting a student who is depressed, anxious or self-harming.

Chapter 6

WE RECOGNISE AND SUPPORT OUR MOST VULNERABLE LEARNERS

Learners can be vulnerable for a whole range of reasons, and in this chapter I invite you to think about how you can recognise and support vulnerable learners in every shape and form. Sometimes it's the students you least expect who most need some additional support.

Success for the most vulnerable is success for all

Over the years I've learnt that if we're able to create an environment that enables our most vulnerable learners to flourish, then we've created an environment in which every learner can flourish. For example, when I'm preparing to teach about sensitive subjects, I always imagine that front row and centre is sat somebody who's been personally affected by the topic in hand. When my lesson development and delivery bears that person in mind, it makes the lesson safe and sensitive not only to their needs, but to the needs of the whole class.

Many fly under the radar

Vulnerability can be masked or hidden for a number of reasons and we're often unaware of the range of vulnerabilities within our class, perhaps because this information hasn't been shared with us, or perhaps because this information hasn't been shared at all. Sometimes vulnerable learners will work very hard to go unnoticed and others aren't even aware that their experiences are unusual in any way – if things have always been a certain way for them, young children especially will often assume that this is the lived reality of everyone around them too.

'My home was one where I felt constantly scared. But I thought that was normal. When I look back, it's unbelievable what I believed was normal, but it was MY normal, so I assumed it was normal for everyone.'

A small amount of support can make a big difference

Taking steps to recognise and support students in need of additional support for whatever reason can have a huge impact on their ability to engage with and enjoy their school life. A pair of school shoes, sanitary towels or writing equipment might make the difference between a child attending school or not, whilst for another child having an adult stop and listen to them for just a few minutes can help them to feel safe and cared for. Sometimes the smallest actions make the biggest difference to children most in need.

TRY THIS?

'Set no homework that relies upon having resources at home (paper/internet/quiet space).' @kaymagpie

TAKING A CHILD-CENTRED APPROACH TO SUPPORTING STUDENTS USING ONE-PAGE PROFILES AT THE GIRLS DAY SCHOOL TRUST

Cate Harvey, head of educational support at the Girls Day School Trust, told me about why and how she's started using one-page profiles to enable staff and parents to learn more about, and appropriately support, their students.

We were introduced to the concept of the one-page profile during some Equality Act training earlier this year. One-page profiles were developed by Helen Sanderson as part of her company's transformative person-centred practices. There are templates on her company's website that can be adapted to any setting and they follow three broad areas: a student's best characteristics, what is important to them and how school can support them. (See http://helensandersonassociates.co.uk.)

We thought it was such a powerful tool that we first adapted it to be a questionnaire that every girl in the school filled out with their parents. We called this 'All About Me'. What this facilitated was real parental involvement as they sometimes found out things about their daughters that they hadn't known before or were able to share important things with school that we wouldn't have known if we hadn't asked.

What we then did was to read through each one individually and then collectively decide which ones we would convert into one-page profiles. We adapted Helen Sanderson's template to include two boxes right at the top of the document where we put the girl's best characteristics and what she felt was important to her. We then changed the third box into 'needs' and 'reasonable adjustments' aimed at meeting these needs. At the bottom is a section for the school, parents and the girl to sign after as many discussions as are needed to get the profile right.

For it to work, and ideally to replace individual education plans and provision mapping documentation, it has to be a 'living' page that all have agreed to and that is regularly referred to by all stakeholders and changed as necessary.

So far, it has enabled us to have excellent, open and well-structured meetings with parents and girls where they feel involved and listened to. Where we are still in the 'work in progress' stage is around whole-school staff involvement – in other words, how we communicate its importance to everyone so that they see it as a useful tool to support our girls who need reasonable adjustments without it feeling like it's just another layer of paperwork.

NOTES:

COLLECTING IDEAS:
WE RECOGNISE AND SUPPORT OUR
MOST VULNERABLE LEARNERS

This space is for you to jot down your thoughts and ideas as they arise. I've split it into start, stop, continue and change, which can be a neat way of thinking about the actions we need to take. You might make a few notes of things you learned during the Mentally Healthy School Audit/Go Out And Listen exercise (see the end of Chapter 2) or you could make notes of your ideas as you read this chapter. Revisit this space and keep track of additional ideas as they arise here. It's not meant to be perfect or beautiful, it's just a place to keep your ideas so you can refer to it when you do your action planning.

Things to START doing…

. . . .

. . . .

. . . .

. . . .

. . . .

. . . .

. . . .

. . . .

Things to STOP doing…

. . . .

. . . .

. . . .

. . . .

. . . .

. . . .

. . . .

Things to CONTINUE doing…

. . . .

. . . .

. . . .

. . . .

. . . .

. . . .

. . . .

. . . .

Things to CHANGE our way of doing…

. . . .

. . . .

. . . .

. . . .

. . . .

. . . .

. . . .

. . . .

. . . .

Other notes:

. . . .

. . . .

. . . .

. . . .

. . . .

. . . .

EIGHT PRACTICAL STEPS YOU COULD TAKE

The key is not to take all of these steps, but rather to identify a few that feel like a good fit and to focus on how you might go about achieving those. Use the action plan later in this chapter to help you.

1. Poverty proof your school uniform

Consider whether your school uniform and sports kit are affordable for all families. Being a little flexible and enabling uniform to be purchased from local supermarkets rather than specialist suppliers can make a big difference to families on lower incomes. You could also consider enabling families to sell or pass on their second-hand uniform – if you have an active Parent–Teacher Association, this might be a task they'll willingly take on, both saving money for families and also raising a little income for the school. If students in your school are penalised for incorrect uniform, consider whether this may be unfairly penalising those students from poorer families and how you might be able to unpick the reasons behind uniform violations without causing embarrassment to the student.

2. Hold support groups for young carers

Many young carers do not even realise that they are a young carer. Whilst it's a relatively common role for young people to play, it's one that isn't talked about much. Many young carers simply get on with the additional responsibilities they have, rarely complaining or asking for help. Many young carers are better at supporting others than at looking out for themselves, and their responsibilities at home can sometimes mean they have less time to relax or have fun. Providing young carers with the chance to come together, to talk to other people in a similar situation so that they feel less alone, can be really helpful. These kinds of support groups can help develop the skills of young carers so that they learn about the importance of self-care too – but they can also be a great space to forget all of their responsibilities for a little while and just be a kid.

3. Have a digital safeguarding system to collate concerns

In order to pick up issues with students, it can be helpful to note patterns as they arise. Having a digital system and a lead member of staff can help enable this. Think about the kinds of concerns you'd like to encourage staff to be reporting and when and how you should regularly review this information. Providing a simple way for staff to note even minor concerns about a student's wellbeing can often mean we pick up issues far sooner than we would otherwise – three members of staff noting minor concerns might trigger a response that might otherwise only occur once the situation had escalated enough to cause major concern.

4. Have named staff to support LGBTQ+ students

Having members of staff who'll act as champions for various vulnerable groups can help students know who to talk to if they have concerns about themselves or a friend. In particular, having named champions for LGBTQ+ students and clear information for students about how they can access support or listening from these members of staff can enable a safe space for students to talk through any questions or concerns they may have.

5. Host coffee and chat sessions

Providing a safe space for parents and carers to catch up and support each other can be incredibly helpful. In its most basic form, these sessions don't need to be anything more than a space to have a cuppa and a catch-up after drop-off. If you want to take it further, you could consider holding specific groups for parents facing similar challenges, and you might build on this further by building in some expert input if it's welcomed by the parents. Consider how you can advertise and run these sessions so they feel inviting even to those parents who are reluctant to engage with your school, perhaps because of their own experiences.

6. Run a nurture group

Many schools now run nurture groups to support vulnerable students to develop the social and emotional skills and understanding that they need in order to thrive at school. Nurture groups are typically small group settings which focus on enabling students to feel safe and cared for, and many students are better able to access the mainstream curriculum as a result of spending some time as part of a nurture group. A variation on this includes creating a nurture space, either for the whole school or within individual classrooms, that students can access at times of need.

Consider how students gain access to the nurture group or space – if possible, it is very positive if this can be done proactively to support students ahead of difficulties or meltdowns rather than in response to them.

7. Run a breakfast club

Running a breakfast club has many benefits for student wellbeing and can be a great help to busy parents too, but at its most basic, a breakfast club can help to ensure that no child arrives to school hungry, which many may do otherwise. As well as fulfilling a basic human need, this also aids student concentration and improves behaviour as well as punctuality, as students arrive at school early for the club. If possible, breakfast clubs should be free or subsidised for lower-income families or those students entitled to free school meals – there are sometimes local or national grants to help with this.

Think carefully about the recruitment of students to your breakfast club. A study by the Department for Education about breakfast clubs in England found that they struggled to recruit the students who might benefit the most. The precise reasons for this were unclear, but it is worth being aware of the need to actively engage the families who might most benefit from your breakfast club and consider how to break down any potential social stigma attached to attendance.

8. Have a part-time social worker on staff

Some schools either employ or work closely with a social worker in order to help support vulnerable students and families. The skills and knowledge that a social worker can bring to your school community can be incredibly valuable. Having regular access to a social worker can help with the identification and implementation of support for children and families in need. Social workers can also provide valuable learning opportunities for staff, helping to develop their skills and understanding when working with vulnerable children. Additionally, a social worker will generally have good knowledge of local support networks and can help with referrals to these. Historically, schools have accessed social workers on a needs-must basis, but some schools are reporting that investing time and budget into a more proactive social work or care model is beneficial to students, families and staff.

NOTES:

....

....

....

....

....

....

....

....

....

....

....

....

....

TRY THIS?

'Provide safe dens in the classroom if needed – my little girl (who is on the autistic spectrum) has one and it's fab!' @1tometoday

CREATING A SAFE HAVEN FOR VULNERABLE STUDENTS IN WEST YORKSHIRE

Cath Jackson is assistant head teacher at Kirkburton Middle School in a village in West Yorkshire in the North of England. The school caters for children aged 10 to 14 and has 509 students.

Over the last five years we have become more and more aware of the increasing number of students transferring to our school who have problems forming and maintaining friendships and who need help with their emotional and personal wellbeing. Information from our feeder schools indicates a rise in the number of those students who are considered to be vulnerable and parents have also contacted our school to ask for support with their child's social and emotional development.

As a response to this we decided to alter a bungalow we have on our school site (our old caretaker's house) to provide a dedicated space to support our more vulnerable children. The aim was to provide a supportive, structured, nurturing environment which encouraged social and emotional development. Initially we trained two members of staff to develop a Nurture Group (Acorns) that met in the bungalow every morning and also opened the bungalow at lunchtime (Open Door) so children could meet, have their lunch, play games and socialise together.

Five years on and Acorns and Open Door is one of our successes. Each year the children attending Acorns and Open Door alters depending on their social and emotional needs. This year we have found that Open Door supports the needs of our current cohort of children adequately without the need for Acorns, and former members of Open Door have progressed to happily spending most of their social time with the rest of their peer group.

A member of staff has responsibility for Open Door; they have a budget, organise activities, equip the kitchen and support those children who attend. Over the years Open Door for some children has been the difference in them wanting to attend school or not and has provided them with a much-needed 'safe haven'.

TRY THIS?

'Help teachers understand students' perspectives, e.g. through student voice initiatives, which include the voice of students with additional or special needs.' @deeburf

IDEAS TO CHERRY PICK FROM

Each one of these ideas has worked for someone somewhere – take a look through the list and place a tick against any you think might be worth considering in your setting.

○ Become attachment and trauma aware

○ Appoint outreach or family support workers to support families in need

○ Keep a stash of cereal bars for students who've come to school on an empty stomach

○ Poverty proof your school uniform

○ Become a food bank referrer

○ Encourage a diverse and approachable range of parent governors

○ Some students may fear social workers – consider how to break down these barriers, for example through an informal approach

○ Develop an LGBTQ+ aware approach and actively promote equality

○ Provide free sanitary items to poverty proof periods

○ Run holiday hunger projects (these support students who are in receipt of free school meals in term time but who may go hungry during the holidays)

○ Organise staff so that different staff are responsible for pastoral support and discipline

○ Collaborate with sensory support staff when planning and assessing

○ Have clear, consistent boundaries to make school feel safe and predictable

○ Provide appropriate support for staff so they have the space in their minds for vulnerable students and the capacity to think about what their behaviours (which might be really challenging) might be communicating

○ Have dedicated 'bubble time' in which students can privately discuss any worries with their teachers

○ Consider training up learning mentors and Thrive practitioners – more here: www.thriveapproach. com

ACTION PLAN:
WE RECOGNISE AND SUPPORT OUR
MOST VULNERABLE LEARNERS

	Short-term	**Medium-term**	**Long-term**
Baseline Score	Aim ☐	Aim ☐	Aim ☐
	Date … / … / ……	Date … / … / ……	Date … / … / ……
	Actual ☐	Actual ☐	Actual ☐
	Date … / … / ……	Date … / … / ……	Date … / … / ……

Set yourself a short-term, a medium-term and a longer-term aim of how you'd like to be scoring in this area. Be realistic and try to set achievable goals – you can always revise them up and down if you need to.

WHY DOES IT MATTER?

What are your motivations for working on this area – why does it matter to you and your school now? What difference might working on this area make?

. . . .

. . . .

. . . .

. . . .

. . . .

. . . .

CURRENT STRENGTHS

What is already working well and how can you build on this success?

. . . .

. . . .

. . . .

. . . .

. . . .

CURRENT CHALLENGES

What is stopping you from scoring more highly here and how might you overcome these challenges?

. . . .

. . . .

. . . .

. . . .

. . . .

. . . .

. . . .

AIM 1: A QUICK WIN – CHOOSE SOMETHING YOU CAN DO RIGHT AWAY TO MAKE A DIFFERENCE

. . . .

. . . .

. . . .

. . . .

. . . .

. . . .

. . . .

WHY?

Why are you setting this aim?

. . . .

. . . .

. . . .

. . . .

. . . .

. . . .

. . . .

WHO?
Who needs to be responsible, involved or persuaded?

. . . .

. . . .

. . . .

. . . .

. . . .

. . . .

. . . .

WHEN?
How long do you need to achieve this aim? How often should you review?

. . . .

. . . .

. . . .

. . . .

. . . .

. . . .

. . . .

HOW?
How will you achieve this aim – what actions need to be taken?

. . . .

. . . .

. . . .

. . . .

. . . .

. . . .

. . . .

WHAT?
What would success look like? What will be the impact? How will you measure it?

. . . .

. . . .

. . . .

. . . .

. . . .

. . . .

. . . .

REVIEW DATE: . . . .

REVIEW NOTES:

. . . .

. . . .

. . . .

. . . .

. . . .

. . . .

. . . .

. . . .

. . . .

. . . .

. . . .

. . . .

. . . .

. . . .

AIM 2: A MEDIUM-TERM GOAL – WHAT CAN YOU AIM TO DO WITHIN THE NEXT THREE MONTHS?

....

....

....

....

....

....

....

WHY?
Why are you setting this aim?

....

....

....

....

....

....

....

WHO?
Who needs to be responsible, involved or persuaded?

....

....

....

....

....

....

....

....

WHEN?
How long do you need to achieve this aim? How often should you review?

....

....

....

....

....

....

....

HOW?
How will you achieve this aim – what actions need to be taken?

....

....

....

....

....

....

....

WHAT?
What would success look like? What will be the impact? How will you measure it?

....

....

....

....

....

....

REVIEW DATE: . . . .

REVIEW NOTES:

. . . .

. . . .

. . . .

. . . .

. . . .

. . . .

. . . .

. . . .

. . . .

. . . .

. . . .

. . . .

. . . .

. . . .

. . . .

. . . .

. . . .

. . . .

. . . .

. . . .

. . . .

AIM 3: A LONGER-TERM CHALLENGE – WHAT IS GOING TO TAKE SIX MONTHS TO A YEAR TO ACHIEVE IF YOU START WORK ON IT RIGHT AWAY?

....

....

....

....

....

....

....

WHY?
Why are you setting this aim?

....

....

....

....

....

....

....

WHO?
Who needs to be responsible, involved or persuaded?

....

....

....

....

....

....

....

WHEN?

How long do you need to achieve this aim? How often should you review?

. . . .

. . . .

. . . .

. . . .

. . . .

. . . .

. . . .

HOW?

How will you achieve this aim – what actions need to be taken?

. . . .

. . . .

. . . .

. . . .

. . . .

. . . .

. . . .

WHAT?

What would success look like? What will be the impact? How will you measure it?

. . . .

. . . .

. . . .

. . . .

. . . .

. . . .

REVIEW DATE: . . . .

REVIEW NOTES:

. . . .

. . . .

. . . .

. . . .

. . . .

. . . .

. . . .

. . . .

. . . .

. . . .

. . . .

. . . .

. . . .

. . . .

. . . .

. . . .

. . . .

. . . .

. . . .

. . . .

BECOMING A TRAUMA INFORMED SCHOOL – EXPERT ADVICE FROM BETSY DE THIERRY

Betsy de Thierry, a qualified psychotherapist and primary school teacher, founded the Trauma Recovery Centre and is the author of the *Simple Guide to Child Trauma*. I asked Betsy to explain why it's important for schools to become trauma informed, and what practical steps they could take.

Becoming a trauma informed school is vital because we now recognise that one in three diagnosed mental health problems in adulthood are known to directly relate to childhood traumatic experiences. A trauma informed school is a school that has chosen to learn how to respond to those children who have experienced trauma in a way that reduces the short-term and long-term impact on their wellbeing.

Trauma impacts a child's behaviour, learning, emotions, relationships and memory. Trauma can be defined as any experience where a child feels simultaneously terrified and powerless and is unable to immediately experience comfort and safety from an adult who can help them make sense of the overwhelming experience. Here are some other definitions:

> A psychologically distressing event that is outside the range of usual human experience, often involving a sense of intense fear, terror and helplessness. (Perry, 2014)[1]

> Trauma happens when any experience stuns us like a bolt out of the blue; it overwhelms us, leaving us altered and disconnected from our bodies. Any coping mechanisms we may have had are undermined, and we feel utterly helpless and hopeless. It is as if our legs are knocked out from under us. (Levine and Kline, 2010)[2]

Trauma symptoms can vary from aggression, emotional volatility, self-harm, wetting and soiling, to being withdrawn, being compliant, angry outbursts, running out of the classroom, having panic attacks, being overly clingy with an adult, not being able to engage in learning, and being day-dreamy and agitated. Children can recover from the impact of trauma when they feel emotionally safe and connected to an adult who enables them to process the experience. Trauma cannot be processed through words as the area of the brain responsible for thinking and reflection (the pre-frontal cortex) and the area of the brain responsible for speech and language (Broca's area) has reduced neural activity and essentially 'goes offline' because the brain becomes focused on surviving the threat and terror.

---

1   Perry, B.D. (2014) *Helping Traumatized Children: A Brief Overview for Caregivers*. Caregiver Series. Houston: The ChildTrauma Academy.

2   Levine, P.A. and Kline, M. (2010) *Trauma Through a Child's Eyes: Awakening the Ordinary Miracle of Healing*. Berkeley: North Atlantic Books.

We know that behaviour is communication. The acting-out behaviour such as aggression, disruption and volatility, or the acting-in behaviour such as self-loathing, being withdrawn or not focusing on learning, all tell us that the child has needs that are not being met. Adults in schools can provide warm, genuine, consistent, caring, kind, nurturing relationships that can help a traumatised child feel emotionally safe, which can lead to them feeling less overwhelmed. This in turn leads them to be less dysregulated in their behaviour because they know who they can turn to, and how, when they need help with a sense of sudden overwhelm in their emotions or nervous system where the impact of trauma resides.

A trauma informed school culture makes sure that adults never ask 'What's wrong with this child?' but always ask 'What happened for them to behave like this?' Trauma recovery focused work is a step further and requires specialist help to enable the traumatised child to fully process their experience. This enables them to live a life where the traumatic experience no longer impacts their every day.

Practical steps to becoming a trauma informed school

1. Make sure the whole school (including lunchtime staff and administrative staff) have been trained to understand that behaviour is communication and that disruptive, challenging behaviour is usually from a child with an unmet need.

2. Make sure all adults remember to ask 'What has happened to them?' rather than 'What's wrong with them?', and then take time to reflect so that empathy is a strong adult approach.

3. Make sure that all staff are helped to be aware of how children show trauma symptoms so that a traumatised child can be identified by their behaviour and reactions and we are not dependent on knowing their story.

4. Create a school culture where blame and shame are not a natural response but rather empathy, kindness and curiosity, from adults to the children and adults to adults.

5. Create a behaviour policy that is not based on a child being able to reflect and be rational when they are overwhelmed, but recognises that a traumatised child needs time with a safe adult to slowly learn how to reflect and understand consequences. Reward and punishment behaviour policies and practices create increased stress and escalation of overwhelm for traumatised children.

6. Despite budget restraints, having staff trained and available to be the safe adults in a school, and ready for a traumatised child to need to be with them, reduces cost in the long term.

7. Help all children understand the impact of trauma on humans. Teaching them the physiological response to terror and how it can make us all have 'muddled brains' can reduce bullying and frustration and instead help children develop empathy and kindness which leads to short- and long-term healthy communities.

8. Have calm, safe and sensory areas for anyone to access when they feel overwhelmed. I assure you that healthy children won't want to be there after a short while as they would rather learn!

9. Invest in supporting parents and communicating without shame and blame so that they can inform the school of information that enables the staff to help the children with their overwhelm and fear.

10. Provide books and training regularly to enable teachers to realise what an extraordinary role they have, how they are changing lives and how they need to look after themselves as they look after the children in their care.

More can be found in *Teaching the Child on the Trauma Continuum* (2015, Grosvenor Publishing) and *The Simple Guide to Child Trauma* (2016, Jessica Kingsley Publishers) and on the websites www.trc-uk.org and www.betsytraininguk.co.uk.

FURTHER READING

Addressing Adversity by YoungMinds

This e-book was commissioned by Health Education England and consists of evidence, insight and case studies from leading experts, clinicians, commissioners and frontline professionals to raise awareness about the impact of adversity and trauma on the mental health of young people (including a chapter written by yours truly). It's big and dense and some chapters are more useful than others, but if you want to get a better understanding of the range of challenges young people might face and what the evidence suggests we can do to support them, then it's a good place to start.

It's free to download via the YoungMinds website: http://youngminds.org.uk/ addressingadversity.

Chapter 7

PARENTS AND CARERS POSITIVELY ENGAGE WITH MY SCHOOL

Engaging parents and carers in a meaningful way is something that sets some schools apart from others. It's not easy, and I've been really impressed by the innovative approaches that some schools I've worked with have taken in order to get this right, so I've shared some of their ideas in this chapter because, whilst parental engagement may be difficult, it really does reap dividends when done well. Wherever I refer to parents, I mean parent, carer or guardian – whoever has a caring responsibility for a child.

Team around the child

At the end of the day, we all want every child to thrive and succeed; this is most likely to happen when we're able to work together as a true team around the child. Where parents and carers feel that lines of communication with the school are open and honest and that they can ask for support when needed and let the school know when there are difficulties outside of school that might impact on a child, then we are all in a better position to support the children in our care.

> 'We're all on the same team – all we want is what's best for the child. When we are open and honest in our discussions and always make sure that the child's best interests are at the heart of our decisions, everybody wins – most especially the child.'

TRY THIS?

'One of the schools I am in have a parents' room. It's a nice comfortable room that the parent teacher association (PTA) can do their work in but also for parents just to have a cuppa after dropping kids off.' @rodey_82

Parenting is hard

There is also a lot that parents can learn from the skills and experience of school staff. Parenting is a difficult and often lonely task, so the opportunity to learn from fellow parents and from professionals at school can be valuable indeed if it is approached in the right way. This isn't about us and them – it's about us all working together with the best interests of the child at the heart of our thoughts and deeds.

Promoting the wellbeing of students and parents

As well as supporting parents to support their children, sometimes it's the parents themselves who are in need of support or signposting. Traditionally this would be seen as beyond the school's remit, but increasingly I talk to schools who feel they have a responsibility to support the wellbeing of parents and carers too, not least because providing or signposting the right support to vulnerable parents can have a direct impact on the wellbeing of students too.

TRY THIS?

'Refer to me by my title and name, not as "Mum", and ask what we can do together to resolve the issue we are facing.' @sarahjanecritch

ENGAGING PARENTS THROUGH 'PRIDE TIME' AT WOODLAND ACADEMY TRUST

Julie Carson, executive head teacher at Woodland Academy Trust in London, explained the Trust's 'Pride Time' initiative where parents are invited in once a term for their children to share things in the classroom they are proud of.

Working in a school in an area of high deprivation, with low parental engagement and traditionally 'hard to reach' parents, we needed to think of a different way to improve parent–school interactions.

A suggestion was made by one of our parent governors as to how to try and improve this, and this quickly became known as 'Pride Time'.

Pride Time is a time once a term (usually a week or two before parents' evening) where parents come in to school in the morning alongside their children, and the children share aspects of their work in the classroom they are proud of and discuss it with their parents. Parents are asked to complete a speech bubble alongside their child to find something to praise, which is then displayed in school to remind children of the amazing work they are doing. The time is also a way of introducing our families to aspects of school 'by stealth'. For instance, if we ran a traditional workshop on our new handwriting scheme, we would only reach approximately 5 per cent of our families across the school. By each class having a handwriting demonstration during Pride Time, we would reach at least 60 per cent of our families across the school. It also enables some of our families to be specifically targeted by senior leaders or our inclusion team if we know they have particular animosity towards school or need support in some way. Those 'while you are here, have you seen…' conversations are particularly useful.

Even though Pride Time is advertised well in advance, we also ask the children to write to their family to invite them to the event – we have found child-power is far stronger than a hundred reminders from us!

Since introducing Pride Time, we have significantly increased parental engagement within our school. Children love spending time with their family member discussing their work, and this has positively impacted on their wellbeing. Families have reported an increased understanding as to what work their children are doing, and also how much more confident they feel about coming in to school to engage in and discuss unrelated matters. As I moved schools, I introduced Pride Time at my new school, and it has also worked incredibly well in a second setting.

If you'd like to introduce Pride Time in your school, here are my suggestions on potential barriers and how to overcome them:

- *Working parents being able to access this* – by advertising the dates on the annual calendar at the beginning of each year, most families are able to attend. If they can't, be flexible; for example we had a couple of families request they attend after school instead.

- *Some children feeling left out as their families could not attend* – staff sat with these children and shared work, including the senior leadership team, so this was not an issue.

- *Some parents not being able to record their thoughts on the speech bubble* – by asking the children and their grown-up to write it together, this enables the child to scribe for their parent.

- *Having more than one child in the school* – this is still an aspect we have not quite solved! The family member moves between classes to share work with each child, but this means they spend less time with each child. We have considered having different mornings for different classes, but this potentially impacts too much on working families.

- *Parents being negative on the speech bubbles* – we model the speech bubbles at the beginning of each year and remind parents of the purpose of them – to share positive aspects they are pleased with, not to identify next steps.

TRY THIS?

'We hold a six-week-in breakfast for parents of September starters. We also hold a coffee morning to ask what works well and what needs improving and a grandparents' afternoon tea to get them on board.' @pixtink

COLLECTING IDEAS:
PARENTS AND CARERS POSITIVELY
ENGAGE WITH MY SCHOOL

This space is for you to jot down your thoughts and ideas as they arise. I've split it into start, stop, continue and change, which can be a neat way of thinking about the actions we need to take. You might make a few notes of things you learned during the Mentally Healthy School Audit/Go Out And Listen exercise (see the end of Chapter 2) or you could make notes of your ideas as you read this chapter. Revisit this space and keep track of additional ideas as they arise here. It's not meant to be perfect or beautiful, it's just a place to keep your ideas so you can refer to it when you do your action planning.

Things to START doing…

. . . .

. . . .

. . . .

. . . .

. . . .

. . . .

. . . .

. . . .

Things to STOP doing…

. . . .

. . . .

. . . .

. . . .

. . . .

. . . .

. . . .

Things to CONTINUE doing…

. . . .

. . . .

. . . .

. . . .

. . . .

. . . .

. . . .

. . . .

Things to CHANGE our way of doing…

. . . .

. . . .

. . . .

. . . .

. . . .

. . . .

. . . .

. . . .

Other notes:

. . . .

. . . .

. . . .

. . . .

. . . .

EIGHT PRACTICAL STEPS YOU COULD TAKE

The key is not to take all of these steps, but rather to identify a few that feel like a good fit and to focus on how you might go about achieving those. Use the action plan later in this chapter to help you.

1. Allow families to join for school lunch

Some schools allow parents, carers and siblings to join their child and their friends for lunch on an ongoing basis; others hold family lunches on special occasions such as Mother's Day or Father's Day. This can help to break down the school–home divide and give families a glimpse into their child's life at school. You can invite wider family members too – one school I spoke to during the research for this book regularly holds a grandparents' tea.

2. Think about the needs of parents who have work or childcare commitments

Whenever you are considering inviting parental involvement with school, consider the needs of working parents or those with younger children at home. There are many simple steps you can take to improve engagement such as considering the timing of events, having an onsite creche or livestreaming or recording talks and making them available online.

3. Involve children in parental engagement activities

Parents and carers are more likely to attend events where their child plays a part – and also students often have a great insight into what they think it would be beneficial for their parents to know or understand, so this is a win–win.

4. Have a parent section on your school website

At its most basic this might highlight important information or policies that parents need to be aware of. You can build on this by providing information about what students are covering at school, particularly where parents might be able to build on this learning at home; perhaps consider a few key questions that parents might explore with their children. You can also use the school website to highlight sources of support and information for families which they might not otherwise be aware of.

5. Create a parent space or room

If you have the space to do so, have a dedicated parent and carer space in your school. This can help parents to feel more welcome in the school and can be a good place to share resources and information. It doesn't need to be anywhere too flashy; somewhere with a few noticeboards and room for tea and chat works very well. If you have one, your Parent–Teacher Association might like to take the lead on creating and utilising this space.

6. Hold induction sessions for parents of new starters

Parents are most likely to engage with school when their child has recently started. They often have lots of questions and are keen to ensure their child gets off to the best start. Try to engage parents and carers at this stage in such a way that they are more likely to continue to engage by holding induction sessions that are both enjoyable and helpful. A few weeks into the new school year you might hold a breakfast, a coffee morning or an evening workshop for parents of new starters. As well as providing information and answering their questions, you could actively explore with them how the school can best engage with them in future. Are there particular issues they'd like input on, are there better times or formats for workshop delivery and would they prefer to be contacted in a particular way?

7. Consider how to engage split and blended families

Consider how you can engage all parents and carers involved with a child's upbringing in a way that is beneficial to a child. Proactively engage with students or families to find out whether duplicates of school newsletters, reports and so forth should be shared with more than one household. Consider too about how best to share information about parent workshops or engagement events.

8. Directly engage parents in student learning

Consider whether there are any specific ways you can engage parents and carers with a child's learning, either through the tasks they take home or by actively inviting them into school.

NOTES:

....

....

....

....

....

....

....

....

....

....

....

....

....

....

TRY THIS?

'Consider how to engage split and blended families. I've lost count of the assemblies and concerts we've missed because school only communicate with one parent or have a ticket rationing system that means no one wins, especially the child.' @jobartkirklees

ESTABLISHING A PARENT COUNCIL AT ST NICHOLAS CHURCH OF ENGLAND PRIMARY ACADEMY IN KENT

Jenny Ross, chair of St Nicholas' parent council, talks about why and how a parent council was introduced and the steps you could take to develop a parent council in your school.

In 2014, following a school inspection, St Nicholas was graded inadequate and in the lowest 10 per cent nationally. Staff turnover was high and the school suffered from low parental engagement. Since the appointment of the current head, Mr Dale, in September 2015, the school has been working hard to change this outcome. The need for change was obvious from my perspective. I am passionate about children's welfare and education, having worked as a family support officer in the local children's centre. Additionally, two of my own children attend St Nicholas and my third will be joining them soon, so the motivation was there personally as well as professionally.

The idea for a parent council was initially met with some scepticism in terms of how it would benefit the school. We arranged some low-key advertising via the school newsletter and spoke to a number of parents. Once they understood that it would enable them to have a voice, the question eventually changed from 'What is it?' to 'How can I be a part of it?'

In the early days, although we were united in wanting to help the school somehow, I think our meetings were too formal. The hall was too big and cold, the circle formation didn't feel right and it was more difficult for members of the council to speak up. Initially, numbers were low and we felt that we weren't reaching as many parents as we had hoped. However, as word spread and we increased communication to staff and parents, numbers began to increase. Our meetings are now more relaxed and less formal, held in the staffroom with tea and cake, which encourages whole-group participation. We now have two signage boards in school, which give us a greater presence. They're a really useful way of removing the 'mystery' and explaining who we are and what we do. We also have two note-takers and two administrative assistants.

Mr Dale and I attended training through 'ParentKind' (www.parentkind.org.uk); it was a great opportunity to meet with other school representatives and we have since developed a partnership link with a school in Surrey, which is similar in size to St Nicholas. One of our note-takers and I visited the school and we are looking to set up a reciprocal visit in the near future, to share ideas and support each other.

The parent council has been really successful in giving parents a voice. It has been highlighted to us that sometimes parents hadn't felt comfortable taking their concerns to teachers, either because they lack the confidence or because they feel that their concern isn't significant enough. We're a way to bridge the gap and provide that vital link between parents and school. We've seen a practical impact, such as changes to the pen licence policy, following feedback from parents. (Pen licences formalise the transition from pencil to ink for young learners who are progressing with their handwriting skills.)

We are currently in the process of starting the school's new 'Friends of St Nicholas'/PTFA (Parents, Teachers and Friends Association) and we're also supporting other schools with the start-up of their very own parent councils.

St Nicholas has had a difficult journey but the school is turning that around. Our parent council has proven that positive relationships help everyone and wellbeing within the school has increased as a consequence.

How you could start your own parent council

- Start softly with your approach and make clear guidelines as to what the council is all about. We are not governors or fundraisers. We are the voice of the parents aiming to help improve the school.

- Shadow a school with an existing parent council. Ask for guidance, copies of minutes or to attend one of their meetings so that you can see how it works.

- Identify any parents that have an interest in the school or a background that would be useful to have on board and spread the word.

- Identify the structure and identify 'openings'. For example, we have two representatives per class. Some larger secondary schools have individual year group councils and allow all parents from that year group to attend. Each school can vary depending on their own structure.

- Make sure teachers, staff, governors, teaching assistants and trusts all know about the council and who the chairperson and members are. It is so important to build up a trusting relationship.

- Invite the council members in. We have had two school dinner days. We lined up and sat amongst the children in the dinner hall to find out what the food is like and how lunch times run.

- Once established, invite members to attend a staff meeting so that members can meet their dedicated teacher.

TRY THIS?

'Focus on small, useful workshops. I've attended many "workshops" at my children's schools, but they are for the whole year group, and it's just a PowerPoint presentation. Workshops should give the parent skills they can apply at home.' @ktclifford10

TRY THIS?

'Our elementary school uses SeeSaw (a student-driven digital portfolio – see http://web.seesaw.me) to communicate with parents and share pictures in real time. Students use it to show what they've learned in school through projects and videos – it's great for working families.' @BAPsmom612

IDEAS TO CHERRY PICK FROM

Each one of these ideas has worked for someone somewhere – take a look through the list and place a tick against any you think might be worth considering in your setting.

- ○ Carry out a parental survey

- ○ Allow parents into classroom at drop-off

- ○ Encourage home–school journals

- ○ Have clear expectations for parents to engage with the school

- ○ Target parents in need and invite them in for specific support/input

- ○ Recognise some parents' school issues resulting from negative childhood experiences

- ○ Contact parents with good news as well as issues

- ○ Hold transition classes for parents

- ○ Take a register at parent events – thank those who came and contact those who didn't with relevant information

- ○ Hold an information evening and invite relevant local third sector organisations in

- ○ Have dedicated 'open door' times for parents with concerns

- ○ Involve children in parental engagement activities

- ○ Give parents tasks, for example accompanying school trips

- ○ Show support to the parent who is dealing with a sick child; this especially applies to children with ongoing health issues

- ○ Offer 'give it a go' weekends for physical activities such as junior park run and encourage family involvement – more here: www.parkrun.org.uk

- ○ Hold parent and child lessons – working together with a teacher on arts/crafts or hands-on science projects

- ○ Hold half-termly parent forums to engage parents in the school improvement process

- ○ Ask parents to help by volunteering with their children to maintain parts of the school grounds such as garden areas or painting/sprucing up tired outdoor equipment

- ○ Have a cuppa and chat group for the parents/carers on those difficult few days when their child is just starting school

- ○ Have a family reading session where you allow parents to come into the classroom and read a book from the class library with their little one

- ○ Appoint 'parents class reps' (separate from the Parent–Teacher Association) to encourage parents to engage with each other and to be another means of parent–school communication

ACTION PLAN:
PARENTS AND CARERS POSITIVELY ENGAGE WITH MY SCHOOL

	Short-term	Medium-term	Long-term
Baseline Score	Aim [ ]	Aim [ ]	Aim [ ]
	Date .../.../.......	Date .../.../.......	Date .../.../.......
	Actual [ ]	Actual [ ]	Actual [ ]
	Date .../.../.......	Date .../.../.......	Date .../.../.......

Set yourself a short-term, a medium-term and a longer-term aim of how you'd like to be scoring in this area. Be realistic and try to set achievable goals – you can always revise them up and down if you need to.

WHY DOES IT MATTER?

What are your motivations for working on this area – why does it matter to you and your school now? What difference might working on this area make?

....
....
....
....
....
....

CURRENT STRENGTHS

What is already working well and how can you build on this success?

....
....
....
....
....

CURRENT CHALLENGES

What is stopping you from scoring more highly here and how might you overcome these challenges?

....

....

....

....

....

....

....

AIM 1: A QUICK WIN – CHOOSE SOMETHING YOU CAN DO RIGHT AWAY TO MAKE A DIFFERENCE

....

....

....

....

....

....

....

WHY?

Why are you setting this aim?

....

....

....

....

....

....

WHO?

Who needs to be responsible, involved or persuaded?

....

....

....

....

....

....

....

WHEN?

How long do you need to achieve this aim? How often should you review?

....

....

....

....

....

....

....

HOW?

How will you achieve this aim – what actions need to be taken?

....

....

....

....

....

....

....

WHAT?

What would success look like? What will be the impact? How will you measure it?

. . . .

. . . .

. . . .

. . . .

. . . .

. . . .

. . . .

REVIEW DATE: . . . .

REVIEW NOTES:

. . . .

. . . .

. . . .

. . . .

. . . .

. . . .

. . . .

. . . .

. . . .

. . . .

. . . .

. . . .

. . . .

. . . .

AIM 2: A MEDIUM-TERM GOAL – WHAT CAN YOU AIM TO DO WITHIN THE NEXT THREE MONTHS?

....

....

....

....

....

....

....

WHY?
Why are you setting this aim?

....

....

....

....

....

....

....

WHO?
Who needs to be responsible, involved or persuaded?

....

....

....

....

....

....

....

WHEN?

How long do you need to achieve this aim? How often should you review?

....

....

....

....

....

....

....

HOW?

How will you achieve this aim – what actions need to be taken?

....

....

....

....

....

....

....

WHAT?

What would success look like? What will be the impact? How will you measure it?

....

....

....

....

....

....

....

REVIEW DATE: ....

REVIEW NOTES:

....

....

....

....

....

....

....

....

....

....

....

....

....

....

....

....

....

....

....

....

....

AIM 3: A LONGER-TERM CHALLENGE – WHAT IS GOING TO TAKE SIX MONTHS TO A YEAR TO ACHIEVE IF YOU START WORK ON IT RIGHT AWAY?

....

....

....

....

....

....

....

WHY?
Why are you setting this aim?

....

....

....

....

....

....

....

WHO?
Who needs to be responsible, involved or persuaded?

....

....

....

....

....

....

....

WHEN?

How long do you need to achieve this aim? How often should you review?

. . . .

. . . .

. . . .

. . . .

. . . .

. . . .

. . . .

HOW?

How will you achieve this aim – what actions need to be taken?

. . . .

. . . .

. . . .

. . . .

. . . .

. . . .

. . . .

WHAT?

What would success look like? What will be the impact? How will you measure it?

. . . .

. . . .

. . . .

. . . .

. . . .

. . . .

REVIEW DATE: . . . .

REVIEW NOTES:

. . . .

. . . .

. . . .

. . . .

. . . .

. . . .

. . . .

. . . .

. . . .

. . . .

. . . .

. . . .

. . . .

. . . .

. . . .

. . . .

. . . .

. . . .

. . . .

. . . .

. . . .

A SMILE IN THE POST WITH GOOD NEWS POSTCARDS IN SWINDON

A SENCO (Special Educational Needs Coordinator) and assistant head of a medium-sized primary and nursery school in an area of deprivation in the UK described how Good News Postcards are helping to bridge the home–school gap.

In 2011, when a new head, new deputy and I took over our respective roles, we identified that we had a significant number of hard-to-reach families. Parents of some of our neediest children were wary of school and nervous of being approached by teachers and school leaders. They were reluctant to engage in any way that would help support their children. In order to tackle this issue we embarked on the Achievement for All (AFA – https://afaeducation.org) programme, and after the first year I took over from the deputy as School Champion for AFA. A couple of years in, our AFA coach mentioned a project she called 'Postcards Home'. I seized this idea and it has run every year since with a huge success rate.

At the beginning of each year we order a volume of postcards with a picture of our school on the front and the following pre-printed on the reverse:

Dear . . . .

I am writing to say that . . . . . .

. . . .

. . . .

Well done!

From

Each teacher is given enough for every child in their class and we give extras to other staff, such as the head and office staff. Whenever a child does something new, kind, different, funny, caring…we write them a postcard and send it home in the post. The real success of this is that the parent and child do not know it is on its way – we have never announced that we do this as a school, so it is always a surprise when the postcard lands on the family doormat in the morning.

We have had parents come in with tears in their eyes thanking us for their child's postcards, genuinely surprised and touched. Children are thrilled and treasure the postcard. This spontaneous way of 'catching the good' has helped parents to understand our ethos and has broken down barriers and opened dialogues that have gone on to make a real difference to our children's academic achievements and emotional wellbeing.

'Postcards Home' is not without its challenges…asking office staff to address 300+ postcards is a big ask, as is expecting busy teachers to look for the good and then remember to write the cards in the midst of the multitude of daily tasks. However, we all recognise the long-term good that these small tokens can do and we all remain committed to continuing this for many years to come.

My tips for success

- Ensure the photo on the postcard is bright, sunny and appealing – maybe featuring a loved part of the school such as play equipment or the hall

- Be creative with who sends them out – for that child who struggles in the classroom a postcard from a lunchtime assistant thanking them for wonderful manners at lunchtime can make them feel six feet tall

- Ensure fairness and equality – don't start a second round until all children in the class have had a postcard; keep careful records of who has had a card and when to help with this

- Planning for delivery on a weekend can help bridge that home–school gap

TRY THIS?

'A school I work in has a parent question per week in the newsletter to seek parental views. It's received well and keeps parents engaged in school and helps them realise that the school values their views. It also makes it easier for the school to address any issues quickly.' @fruitsforest16

FURTHER READING

Engaging Parents – 100 Ideas for Primary Teachers by Jane Goodall and Kathryn Weston (London, 2018)

This book contains advice and ideas on every aspect of parent engagement. Whilst it's aimed primarily at those working in school settings that cater up to age 11, I think that many of the ideas could be adapted for other settings too. The authors have consulted with schools and parents and each of the hundred ideas is clearly explained with helpful hints for making it work and steps for taking the idea further. There's a really wide range of ideas within the unassuming-looking little book – here's a brief taster:

Idea 21: Not all parents are the same – when schools take the time to get to know their parents and families during transition, this is not time wasted. It enables the school to really hit the ground running at the start of term.

Idea 36: Evaluation, evaluation, evaluation – how and why we need to evaluate the engagement events we put on with parents and how we can learn from and build on the successes and challenges we uncover.

Idea 74: It all adds up – parents and maths – this chapter explores why and how to work collaboratively with parents to promote numeracy.

STUDENTS, STAFF AND PARENTS SEEK HELP WHEN NEEDED

Schools where students, staff and parents unashamedly ask for help when it's needed are schools where things are working well, in my view; they are schools where there is no stigma associated with asking for support, where people are confident that if they ask for support they will be heard and helped and where there are clear pathways in place to enable help-seeking.

Help-seeking is an important skill

Help-seeking is an important skill and not just for emotional wellbeing. We need to enable our students to help-seek in a variety of situations – whether it's academic or emotional support they require.

> 'I always make sure I praise my students when they ask for help with their academic work – I figure if they feel comfortable and encouraged asking for help with their school work then they'll feel empowered to ask for help with more difficult issues too.'

Seeking help is a sign of strength

Whilst in some organisations asking for support may be seen as a sign of weakness, in many it is understood as a sign of strength. Being able to recognise that we would benefit from the support of others and proactively seeking that support is both a sign of strength and a means of getting stronger and overcoming whatever issues we're currently facing. Schools where not only students but parents and staff too are proactively encouraged to role model help-seeking are places where the stigma or perceived weakness of not being able to manage alone soon dissipates. This is not to say that we can never be independent – sometimes seeking help means using our independent learning skills to look up an answer or refer to a reference text or website. When we support students to help-seek in a variety of ways in a range of situations, we provide them with the skills and confidence they need to ask for help in more difficult situations.

Help-seeking demonstrates an awareness of support pathways

Students, parents and staff can only seek help if they know where and how to seek help – so when I work with a school where appropriate help-seeking is the norm, I know that this is a school where efforts have been made to raise awareness of the support that is available and how to access it.

NOTES:

....

....

....

....

....

....

....

....

....

....

....

....

....

....

....

....

....

....

COLLECTING IDEAS:
STUDENTS, STAFF AND PARENTS
SEEK HELP WHEN NEEDED

This space is for you to jot down your thoughts and ideas as they arise. I've split it into start, stop, continue and change, which can be a neat way of thinking about the actions we need to take. You might make a few notes of things you learned during the Mentally Healthy School Audit/Go Out And Listen exercise (see the end of Chapter 2) or you could make notes of your ideas as you read this chapter. Revisit this space and keep track of additional ideas as they arise here. It's not meant to be perfect or beautiful, it's just a place to keep your ideas so you can refer to it when you do your action planning.

Things to START doing…

. . . .

. . . .

. . . .

. . . .

. . . .

. . . .

. . . .

. . . .

Things to STOP doing…

. . . .

. . . .

. . . .

. . . .

. . . .

. . . .

. . . .

. . . .

Things to CONTINUE doing...

....

....

....

....

....

....

....

....

Things to CHANGE our way of doing...

....

....

....

....

....

....

....

....

Other notes:

....

....

....

....

....

....

....

EIGHT PRACTICAL STEPS YOU COULD TAKE

The key is not to take all of these steps, but rather to identify a few that feel like a good fit and to focus on how you might go about achieving those. Use the action plan later in this chapter to help you.

1. Teach and reinforce help-seeking skills

From an early age, students can be taught basic help-seeking skills and praised when they engage these skills. This can refer to help-seeking in the broadest sense, not just problems with issues affecting mental health or wellbeing. Students who engage with help-seeking and feel confident asking for and receiving support in an academic context are more likely to transfer this skill to other contexts if needed.

It can also be helpful to explore the role of friends – sometimes friendship means talking to a trusted adult when you're worried about a friend, even if they've asked you not to tell anyone. Explore with students the role of a friend, when we might need to break confidence and what the short- and long-term implications of this might be.

'I swore my friend to secrecy, but he told our form tutor. I was so angry, I didn't speak to him for days – but in the end I was super-grateful. My form tutor was great and he made sure I got the support I needed; he also helped me to realise I had nothing to be ashamed of.'

2. Regularly highlight safe sources of support and encourage critical consumption

When students are in need of support, their first port of call will often be the internet. This is fine as long as they're able to navigate to trusted sources of support. Unfortunately, what can happen sometimes is that they end up on forums or websites which exacerbate the very problem they are seeking help for – this is not uncommon with eating disorders or self-harm where there are many 'pro' sites and forums encouraging unhealthy behaviours. Instead, if we're able to make students aware of trusted websites and helplines, we can increase the likelihood of them finding the help they need. We can also teach more broadly about critical consumption and how to tell a good source of advice from an unreliable one; this could be taught alongside lessons which touch on issues such as fake news.

3. Signpost support in student planners

We can be pretty good at highlighting sources of support as and when we cover specific issues, but we need to remind students of sources of support regularly in case their issues arise at a time that don't fit with our timetable. Additionally, being able to easily access website or helpline information in school planners or on the school's website can enable a student to privately obtain the information they need in order to seek help. This privacy might be important to them if they've not opened up to their peers about the problem in hand.

4. Create student- and parent-friendly versions of policies

Many of our policies will clearly outline referral pathways for students causing concern; however, these policies are rarely read by students or parents and can feel pretty impenetrable. Think about whether it's possible to create student- and/or parent-friendly versions of policies which might be more practical and feel a little more accessible. Policies are often rather turgid and can become a bit of a box-ticking exercise, but if you select one or two policies, work with your students to cut them down and bring them to life and ensure that they are meeting students' needs; this can both act as a reinforcement of referral pathways in and of itself and impact on the future behaviours of students who have clear guidance on when and how to seek help.

'I worked with a school where both staff and students were concerned about the rising levels of self-harm. A simple but highly effective step we took was to create a self-harm policy which was highly practical and included clear guidance about what to do and when. Staff and students worked together to ensure that it was fit for purpose and the students created a one-page summary of the policy which summarised the key points in student-friendly language. Staff felt more confident responding to incidents and concerns about self-harm and students felt more able to come forwards as they had a clear idea of what would happen next. The creation of the policy was almost as important as the implementation of it and it was agreed that it should be reviewed regularly and jointly by both staff and students.'

5. Suggest that students design posters

Posters can be a great way to highlight sources of support or other helpful information for students; having students design the posters can ensure that they are perfectly targeted, that they stand out from the sea of posters that may be on your walls – and of course, the design process itself will give students an important opportunity to learn about the information they're sharing.

6. Explore and try to overcome barriers to help-seeking

Hold focus groups or carry out a survey of students, staff and parents to try and understand if there are any specific barriers to help-seeking. These vary from school to school but common ones include:

- Not knowing who to talk to

- A culture of stigma surrounding help-seeking

- Uncertainty over what will happen next

- Not being able to find a chance to talk privately with a trusted member of staff

It's best to go in with an open mind and listen to student, staff and parent concerns and then to consider how best to address these – actively involving students, parents and staff can help to ensure that any solutions you come up with are relevant, practical and embedded.

7. Make it clear what will happen if someone does ask for help

A common barrier to help-seeking is concern over what will happen next. Students often have no idea what will happen if they seek help, and this uncertainty can stop them coming forward. So when we're teaching students about where, how and when to ask for help, we need also to be clear about what will happen as a result. This should include the positive ramifications – that they'll be listened to, never judged and, we hope, provided with some appropriate support. It should also include the thorny issue of confidentiality. We should be honest up front about the fact that it won't always be possible to keep a student's confidence if they're at risk of harm; but we can also use this opportunity to explore why it's in the student's best interest for concerns to be shared. We can also reassure students that we'll let them know exactly who is told what, and when.

8. Staff to remain for a few minutes after teaching about sensitive issues

If we timetable assemblies, tutor periods or lessons which touch on sensitive issues that might give rise to disclosures or concerns from students, it can really help to have a member of staff remain behind after the session so that any students wishing to raise a concern can do so right away.

NOTES:

. . . .

. . . .

. . . .

. . . .

. . . .

. . . .

. . . .

. . . .

. . . .

. . . .

. . . .

. . . .

. . . .

. . . .

. . . .

TRY THIS?

'My children's school gave out business-size cards with information about where to seek support that kids could keep in purses and wallets. My impression was that those that thought they needed it kept it, those that didn't thought it a waste of time!' @lucindapowell

TRY THIS?

'Never underestimate the power of toilet doors – toilets are often a place of refuge for kids who are worried or scared; putting information there about how and where to seek help can be the prompt a child needs to reach out.' Amy Smith

IDEAS TO CHERRY PICK FROM

Each one of these ideas has worked for someone somewhere – take a look through the list and place a tick against any you think might be worth considering in your setting.

- O Share information:

    - Online

    - In student planners

    - In assemblies

    - In relevant lessons

    - On toilet doors

    - On posters

- O Have students design posters

- O Celebrate help-seeking

- O Explore barriers to help-seeking

- O Consider accessibility issues for some

- O Engage students in developing pathways

- O On the school website, include a list of all staff with names, roles and contact details, for example if you have a problem with x contact y, so if parents have concerns they know who to contact

- O Make staff available and visible to parents on a daily basis, for example in the playground at drop-off/pick-up

- O Have all staff trained in spotting and responding to the warning signs of mental health issues

Confidential helplines and chatrooms can provide a valuable stepping stone

It's important we provide information children need in order to seek help from a trusted adult, but it's also important that we acknowledge that not every child in need of support will feel comfortable doing so face to face. For this reason, it can be valuable to also provide information about support that can be sought via helplines or online. These anonymous sources of non-judgemental listening can provide a hugely valuable stepping stone for young people who can practice talking about the issue that is concerning them. They can see how these words feel in their mouth and maybe put them into sentences for the first time, without having to look the person listening in the eye and whilst knowing for certain they'll never have to see or speak to the listener ever again and that their confidence will not be broken. If this conversation is a positive experience, it can often boost a young person's confidence to go on to seek the support of a trusted adult face to face.

RECOMMENDED RESOURCES

MindEd E-learning Portal: MindEd is an online learning portal covering a huge range of mental health issues suitable for all adults working with children. Modules vary from beginner to advanced and most take up to about half an hour to complete. The modules are authored by experts and the project is funded by Health Education England. You can access the portal for free at www.minded.org.uk.

MindEd for Families: this is similar to MindEd but is written for and with parents and carers – a great resource to share with parents/carers. You can access it for free at www.mindedforfamilies.org.uk.

TRY THIS?

'We have a bubble on the classroom door. Students put their name in the bubble if they need support from an adult. We're trying to encourage students to understand that it's okay not to be okay and that they shouldn't be ashamed of asking for help, so it being very visible is intentional. It also means that students are able to be kind to each other if they see that someone is in need of support. These bubbles are on all doors, not just classroom teachers', so students can request a conversation with any member of staff. Our cleaner put her name in the bubble the other day and was able to get the support she needed too.' David Delaney

ACTION PLAN:
STUDENTS, STAFF AND PARENTS
SEEK HELP WHEN NEEDED

	Short-term	**Medium-term**	**Long-term**
Baseline Score	Aim [ ]	Aim [ ]	Aim [ ]
	Date .../.../......	Date .../.../......	Date .../.../......
	Actual [ ]	Actual [ ]	Actual [ ]
	Date .../.../......	Date .../.../......	Date .../.../......

Set yourself a short-term, a medium-term and a longer-term aim of how you'd like to be scoring in this area. Be realistic and try to set achievable goals – you can always revise them up and down if you need to.

WHY DOES IT MATTER?
What are your motivations for working on this area – why does it matter to you and your school now? What difference might working on this area make?

....

....

....

....

....

....

CURRENT STRENGTHS
What is already working well and how can you build on this success?

....

....

....

....

....

CURRENT CHALLENGES

What is stopping you from scoring more highly here and how might you overcome these challenges?

....

....

....

....

....

....

....

AIM 1: A QUICK WIN – CHOOSE SOMETHING YOU CAN DO RIGHT AWAY TO MAKE A DIFFERENCE

....

....

....

....

....

....

....

WHY?

Why are you setting this aim?

....

....

....

....

....

....

....

WHO?
Who needs to be responsible, involved or persuaded?

. . . .

. . . .

. . . .

. . . .

. . . .

. . . .

. . . .

WHEN?
How long do you need to achieve this aim? How often should you review?

. . . .

. . . .

. . . .

. . . .

. . . .

. . . .

. . . .

HOW?
How will you achieve this aim – what actions need to be taken?

. . . .

. . . .

. . . .

. . . .

. . . .

. . . .

. . . .

WHAT?
What would success look like? What will be the impact? How will you measure it?

....
....
....
....
....
....
....

REVIEW DATE: ....

REVIEW NOTES:

....
....
....
....
....
....
....
....
....
....
....
....
....
....
....
....

AIM 2: A MEDIUM-TERM GOAL – WHAT CAN YOU AIM TO DO WITHIN THE NEXT THREE MONTHS?

....

....

....

....

....

....

....

WHY?
Why are you setting this aim?

....

....

....

....

....

....

....

WHO?
Who needs to be responsible, involved or persuaded?

....

....

....

....

....

....

....

WHEN?

How long do you need to achieve this aim? How often should you review?

. . . .

. . . .

. . . .

. . . .

. . . .

. . . .

. . . .

HOW?

How will you achieve this aim – what actions need to be taken?

. . . .

. . . .

. . . .

. . . .

. . . .

. . . .

. . . .

WHAT?

What would success look like? What will be the impact? How will you measure it?

. . . .

. . . .

. . . .

. . . .

. . . .

. . . .

. . . .

REVIEW DATE: . . . .

REVIEW NOTES:

. . . .

. . . .

. . . .

. . . .

. . . .

. . . .

. . . .

. . . .

. . . .

. . . .

. . . .

. . . .

. . . .

. . . .

. . . .

. . . .

. . . .

. . . .

. . . .

. . . .

AIM 3: A LONGER-TERM CHALLENGE – WHAT IS GOING TO TAKE SIX MONTHS TO A YEAR TO ACHIEVE IF YOU START WORK ON IT RIGHT AWAY?

....

....

....

....

....

....

....

WHY?

Why are you setting this aim?

....

....

....

....

....

....

....

WHO?

Who needs to be responsible, involved or persuaded?

....

....

....

....

....

....

....

WHEN?

How long do you need to achieve this aim? How often should you review?

. . . .

. . . .

. . . .

. . . .

. . . .

. . . .

. . . .

HOW?

How will you achieve this aim – what actions need to be taken?

. . . .

. . . .

. . . .

. . . .

. . . .

. . . .

. . . .

WHAT?

What would success look like? What will be the impact? How will you measure it?

. . . .

. . . .

. . . .

. . . .

. . . .

. . . .

. . . .

REVIEW DATE: . . . .

REVIEW NOTES:

. . . .

. . . .

. . . .

. . . .

. . . .

. . . .

. . . .

. . . .

. . . .

. . . .

. . . .

. . . .

. . . .

. . . .

. . . .

. . . .

. . . .

. . . .

. . . .

. . . .

. . . .

CREATING AN ATMOSPHERE WHERE IT'S OK TO REACH OUT FOR HELP IN SOUTH-EAST ENGLAND

Amy Sayer is the mental health and wellbeing lead at Chichester High School in Kent, England.

We have held house assemblies about the importance of discussing mental health and, as a result, we have 70 students who volunteered to be trained as Mental Health Ambassadors by our adult Mental Health First Aiders. These students understand how to refer students, look after their own mental health, and how to talk about mental health in a meaningful and respectful way. This allows them to support students who are struggling with their mental health, and means mental health can be discussed in the same way as physical health in our school community.

We also have a successful 'talking group' which involves our most vulnerable Year 7s (11- and 12-year-olds) meeting once a week with one of our trained Mental Health First Aiders to complete resilience exercises, build their self-esteem, and have a safe space (our beautiful library) to discuss their feelings. This group has been a great success with our most vulnerable students being able to use public transport for the first time, make new friends, and feel more confident in school. It has been so successful that more students have asked to join and it is now being co-led by one of our Year 11 (15- and 16-year-old) Mental Health Ambassadors.

Next year, all Year 7 and 8 students (11–13-year-olds) will be receiving a Mental Health and Wellbeing curriculum which is taught by two adult Mental Health First Aiders. Its aim is to give students information about supporting good mental health and allow them to develop healthy habits which support their wellbeing and resilience to deal with life's challenges.

Chapter 9

NOW WHAT?

This book is designed to be a starting point rather than an end point, giving you a melting pot of ideas and a simple framework for becoming a more mentally healthy school. I hope you've been able to honestly appraise where your current strengths and challenges lie, and you've been able to think about practical steps you can take to build on the strengths and address the challenges.

Revisit the statements often:

* Staff at my school are happy and healthy

* My school feels safe and welcoming

* The voice of every learner is heard and valued

* We recognise and support our most vulnerable learners

* Parents and carers positively engage with my school

* Students, staff and parents seek help when needed

Be honest about what's working and what's not – and keep on talking to your staff, your students and your parent and carer community to determine where more work is needed, and also what successes you should be taking a moment to celebrate. We sometimes forget to stop and celebrate our successes, so I'm going to encourage you to write on these pages yet again, to take a note of what you've achieved as part of this process that you should be proud of...

WHAT IDEAS HAVE WE IMPLEMENTED THAT ARE WORKING WELL?

....
....
....
....
....

WHAT'S THE IMPACT?

....
....
....
....
....

HOW CAN WE MAKE THIS SUSTAINABLE? HOW CAN WE BUILD ON THIS SUCCESS?

....
....
....
....
....

HOW CAN WE MARK OR CELEBRATE THIS?

....
....
....
....
....

You'll note that I don't invite you to rest on your laurels once you see success – when you've tried something and it's had a tangible impact, your next questions should always be 'How can I make this sustainable?' and 'Can I build on this success?'

But, do stop and take pride in the steps you've taken, no matter how big or how small, and remember that the impact of your actions will be felt by your students – often for far longer and in a far more meaningful way than you might ever have imagined.

> 'What made the biggest difference? It was none of the things you expect me to say… it was the teacher who smiled at me every time he passed me in the corridor. That was it. All he did was smile; but I was drowning and his smile was like a life ring.'

THE SCHOOL MENTAL HEALTH AWARD

If you've enjoyed the process of working through this book and you'd like to do more, you might be interested in learning about Leeds Beckett University's School Mental Health Award, which is a framework for supporting schools to develop a truly whole-school approach to mental health. It's an evidence-based framework currently being undertaken by hundreds of schools. Whilst the award originated in the UK, international schools are very welcome to apply – the coaching all takes place remotely via video link, so it doesn't matter if you're five minutes down the road or across the world from your coach.

It takes about 12 months to complete the process, which gives you time to embrace and embed the ideas in the framework and ensure that they're having a genuine impact on the culture and ethos of the school, rather than just acting like a box-ticking exercise. You can be awarded a bronze, silver or gold award, and many schools are opting to continue working with the same coach to work towards gold or silver awards having obtained bronze or silver in Year One.

I must declare a conflict of interest as I'm a coach on the award and work very closely with the excellent team at Leeds Beckett University – I chose to join the team because the School Mental Health Award aligns well with the evidence base and offers excellent value to schools. It's also a process that many schools had waxed lyrical to me about before I finally jumped on board. I hugely value the coaching conversations I have with my schools. The little window I get into the day-to-day life of a wide range of schools and colleges in completely different circumstances and with very different approaches, but all united in wanting to make their schools a better place for the students, staff and parents/carers, is fascinating, humbling and also a lot of fun.

You can learn more about the process here: www.leedsbeckett.ac.uk/schoolmhaward – or you can email schoolmh@leedsbeckett.ac.uk.

GOOD LUCK, THANK YOU AND KEEP IN TOUCH!

Thank you so much for caring enough about becoming a more mentally healthy school to read this book – good luck with the journey and please do let me know how you get on. I have fond imaginings of people tweeting me pictures of their dog-eared copies of this book which have been used and loved and used and loved. Please write all over it and allow the ideas herein to act as a springboard for your own ideas.

Be bold, try new things – continue what works, stop what doesn't... Whatever you do, don't stand still...

Good luck!

Pooky
@PookyH – Twitter and Instagram
pooky@inourhands.com
www.pookyknightsmith.com
www.youtube.com/pookyh

Index

from the same author

Self-Harm and Eating Disorders in Schools
A Guide to Whole-School Strategies and Practical Support

224pp
Paperback
ISBN: 978 1 84905 584 0
eIBSN: 978 1 78450 031 3

Self-harm and eating disorders are present in almost every school and they frequently co-occur. This book provides the vital guidance that school staff need to spot early warning signs, understand triggers and support the students in their care effectively.

This very practical guide helps educational professionals to gain a better understanding of self-harm and eating disorders by dispelling the myths and misconceptions that surround these behaviours. The book provides advice on whole-school policies and procedures as well as day-to-day strategies to implement in lessons, at mealtimes and in one-on-one sessions. It explains how to respond to disclosures, make referrals and work alongside parents to assist in the road to recovery.

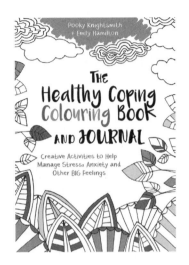

The Healthy Coping Colouring Book
Creative Activities to Help Manage Stress, Anxiety and Other Big Feelings

208pp
Paperback
ISBN: 978 1 78592 139 1
eIBSN: 978 1 78450 405 2

Packed full of creative activities and coping strategies, this journal and colouring book is the perfect companion when faced with difficult thoughts and feelings. Whether you are stressed out at home or school, feeling anxious or simply in need of some relaxation, this workbook provides a place for you to express your emotions. Put your own personal stamp on colouring, journaling and drawing activities and explore healthy ways of coping with difficult feelings such as anger and anxiety through inspirational quotes, poems and practical advice.

With a range of activities that introduce mindfulness and encourage relaxation, this workbook will help young people aged 8–14 to develop the tools needed to prepare for and respond to future difficult situations. It is also an invaluable resource for parents and carers, teachers, counsellors and psychologists to use with young people in their care.

of related interest

You Can Change the World!
Everyday Teen Heroes Making a Difference Everywhere
Margaret Rooke

320pp
Paperback
ISBN: 978 1 78592 502 3
eIBSN: 978 1 78450 897 5

This inspirational book tells the stories of more than 50 of today's teenagers who've dared to change their own lives and the world they live in. They explain how to survive in a world often obsessed by celebrities, social media and what you look like, by refusing to conform to other people's expectations. *If you want to achieve against the odds and create genuine impact, this is the book you need.*

Bestselling author Margaret Rooke asks teens about their experience of being volunteers, social entrepreneurs and campaigners, online and beyond. You'll hear from a young carer of the year; a boy with Down's syndrome, bullied at school, now a successful actor; and a teen who broke his spine on his 15th birthday whose injury taught him to help others. The interviews cover race, sexuality, violence, grief, dyslexia, autism, the environment, the power of music and other issues central to teenage life today.

Margaret Rooke writes books to inspire children, teenagers, their parents and people who work with them, including *Creative, Successful Dyslexic* and *Dyslexia is My Superpower (Most of the Time)*.

My Anxiety Handbook
Getting Back on Track
Sue Knowles, Bridie Gallagher and Phoebe McEwen

192pp
Paperback
ISBN: 978 1 78592 440 8
eIBSN: 978 1 78450 813 5

Helping young people with anxiety learn to recognise and manage their symptoms, this anxiety survival guide teaches young people aged 10+ how they can overcome their biggest worries.

Showing that anxiety is a normal human emotion that many people face, this book helps young people understand the ins and outs of their own anxiety and helps them to challenge the difficult patterns they may get into. Co-written with a college student who has experienced anxiety herself, it is a relatable and straightforward guide. As well as providing tried-and-tested advice and exercises that are proven to reduce feelings of anxiety, it includes recovery stories from young people who have managed their symptoms successfully.

With practical chapters on sleep, exam stress, transitions, and seeking extra help, this is a go-to guide for any tween, teen or young person living with anxiety.

Dr Sue Knowles is a senior clinical psychologist with longstanding experience of working with young people and their carers in a range of settings. She works for the psychological services organisation Changing Minds UK [www.changingmindsuk. com].

Dr Bridie Gallagher is a senior clinical psychologist working with adolescents in acute inpatient environments and secure welfare accommodation. She also teaches on the Leeds and Lancaster clinical psychology doctorate courses.

Phoebe McEwen is a college student with lived experience of anxiety.

The Mental Health and Wellbeing Workout for Teens
Skills and Exercises from ACT and CBT for Healthy Thinking
Paula Nagel

160pp
Paperback
ISBN: 978 1 78592 394 4
eIBSN: 978 1 78450 753 4

This easy-to-understand, engaging guide arms you with healthy thinking habits and coping strategies for staying on top of your mental health. Using tried and tested therapeutic techniques, readers are given the tools to build their own personalised mental health 'workout' to boost their emotional resilience and wellbeing.

Informed by the experiences of other teens, this friendly guide gives practical tips and strategies on how to overcome everyday stresses and ditch negative thinking 'frenemies' before they develop into more serious issues. It also helps you recognise negative thoughts and emotions, explains how you can monitor your mood and behaviour and flex your positive thinking muscles in order to combat the mental health blips we all sometimes face.

Paula Nagel is the principal educational psychologist for a national children's mental health charity. She has 20 years' experience as an educational psychologist, working to promote emotional wellbeing and positive mental health in young people.